> God bless you
> M. Teresa mc

Sri Chinmoy with Mother Teresa
Missionaries of Charity House
Bronx, New York
17 June 1997

(Mother Teresa offers her blessings to Sri Chinmoy as he presents her
with the first part of this book on 17 June 1997)

MOTHER TERESA: HUMANITY'S FLOWER-HEART
DIVINITY'S FRAGRANCE-SOUL

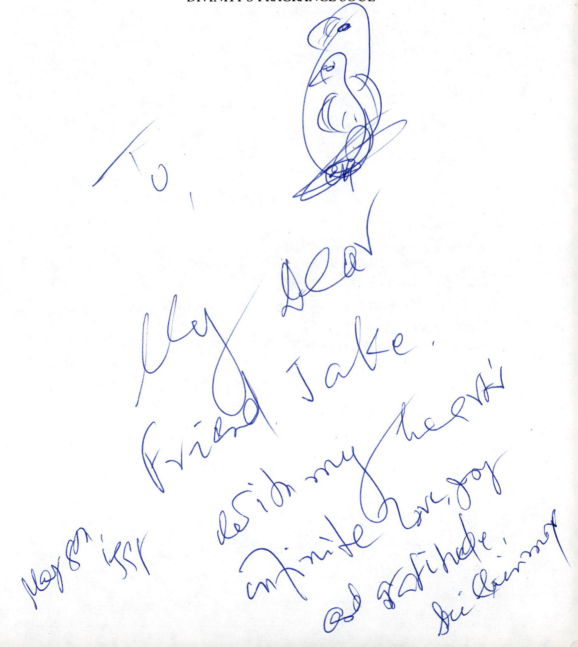

To,
My dear
Friend Jake.
May 8 1994   Deep in my heart's
            infinite love, joy
            and gratitude.
            Sri Chinmoy

SELECTED TITLES BY SRI CHINMOY
───────────────────────────────

Diana, Princess of Wales
   Diana, Empress of the World

India, My India

God Is…

The Wings of Joy

Heart-Songs

The Garland of Nation-Souls

Garden of the Soul

Meditation: Man-Perfection in God-Satisfaction

Beyond Within

The Three Branches of India's Life-Tree:
   Commentaries on the Vedas, the Upanishads and the
   Bhagavad Gita

My Life's Soul-Journey

Inner and Outer Peace

Eastern Light for the Western Mind

Mother Teresa:
Humanity's Flower-Heart
Divinity's Fragrance-Soul

Sri Chinmoy

AGNI PRESS
NEW YORK

The bird drawings in this book are selected from Sri Chinmoy's "Dream-Freedom-Peace-Bird" series.

Copyright © 1997 Sri Chinmoy

All rights reserved. No portion of this book may be reproduced in any form without express written permission from the Publisher.

ISBN: 1-885479-08-5

Agni Press
84-47 Parsons Blvd.
Jamaica, NY 11432 USA
1997
Printed in the USA

Dedication

This book is my heart's prayerful offering
to Mother Teresa
on the most auspicious occasion of her
87th Birthday this year.
Her natural Birthday falls on August 26th.
To my greatest surprise and joy,
her supernatural Birthday,
her baptismal day,
falls on August 27th,
which happens to be my own Birthday.
My Birthday-heart bows and bows and bows
to Mother's Birthday-Soul.

— Sri Chinmoy
17 June 1997

This is the dedication page as it appeared in the book that
was originally given to Mother Teresa by Sri Chinmoy on June 17th.
Sri Chinmoy was inspired to give it to Mother on
that day and not to wait until her actual birthday on August 27th.

CONTENTS

Preface

PART ONE

God's Own Autograph
Poems Dedicated to Mother Teresa 1

A Cosmopolitan Heart
Reflections on Mother Teresa's Life and Words 37

"Are You Praying for Me?"
Treasured Meetings, Selected Telephone Conversations and Letters 49

All-Conquering Compassion
Song-Offerings to Mother Teresa 187
Songs and Meditations on the Saviour Christ 205
In Praise of Mother Mary 227
A Song Dedicated to Pope Paul VI 237
A Song Dedicated to Pope John Paul II 241

PART TWO

Swimming in the Sea of Tears
The News of Mother Teresa's Passing 247

Calcutta's Soaring Bird
A Week of Prayerful Observances 257

Mother Teresa: The Proof of God's Love
Selected Tributes from World Leaders 289

A Common Love of Humanity
*Peace Concert Dedicated to Mother Teresa at the
United Nations* 307

My Mother of Compassion and My Sister of Affection
Loving Reflections about Mother Teresa 313

Mother Teresa-Charity-Critics Are Mental Cases!
The Concept of Charity 387

Postscript: A Letter from Sister Nirmala 395

Preface

Sri Chinmoy began work on this book in June 1997. Mother Teresa's 87th birthday was approaching on 27 August, and he was inspired to write a special series of poems for her. Prompted by an inner sense of urgency, Sri Chinmoy completed the book in time for his last meeting with her on 17 June. His meeting took place in New York, shortly before Mother returned to Calcutta. Mother happily received this early birthday present and offered her written blessings on Sri Chinmoy's own copy.

Over the next few months, Sri Chinmoy expanded the book to include the transcript and photos from their last meeting, as well as the special telephone conversation they had on their shared birthday—27 August.

On 5 September, while Sri Chinmoy was in Warsaw, Poland, to offer a Peace Concert, he received the saddest news of Mother Teresa's passing. Part Two of this book contains his eulogy for Mother Teresa, his messages of sympathy to Sister Nirmala and the Sisters of the Missionaries of Charity, as well as several interviews in which he reflects on Mother Teresa's life and work.

For Sri Chinmoy personally, this living saint of our times will always remain "My Mother of compassion and my Sister of affection."

Part One

God's Own Autograph

POEMS DEDICATED TO
MOTHER TERESA

Mother prays for world peace.

My sisters and brothers of the world,
Are we so blind that we cannot see
God's own Autograph
On Mother Teresa's forehead?

Mother,
To be in your blessingful presence
   Is to breathe in
A breath of living compassion.

GODS'S OWN AUTOGRAPH

Mother,
A single whisper from you
Has transformed thousands of non-believers
And disbelievers.

If any dying sufferer on earth
Needs someone to cry for him,
With him and in him,
Then he can unmistakably see
Mother Teresa's all-embracing arms
Faster than the fastest
Approaching him.

To be in the presence of Mother Teresa
Is to establish friendship
With invaluable moments.

Mother Teresa tells us
That the right choice,
And the only choice,
Is the Christ's Compassion-Heart.

Mother Teresa's heart
Shall forever remain untouched
By the shadows of fears and doubts.

With a single glance,
Mother Teresa enlightens
Our crying eyes, searching minds
And aspiring hearts.

Mother Teresa does many, many things
For the betterment of the world,
But when she washes away
The untold sufferings
Of the unloved ones
With her heart's streaming tears—
That is by far the best.

Mother Teresa is
The dreamer of happiness
   In the heart of
Suffering, imprisoned humanity.

GODS'S OWN AUTOGRAPH

When Mother Teresa approaches
   Ill-fated sufferers,
What does she say?
'Do not worry, my child, God is coming.
Indeed, I see in you the living presence
Of Jesus Christ Himself.'

Mother Teresa's life-boat plies
Between the destination-shores
Of her own grandmother-soul
And her own grandchild-heart.

Mother Teresa tells the whole world
That a heart of love
Is infinitely stronger
Than we can ever imagine.

When I look at my compassion-eyes,
I clearly see that my eyes
Can never be filled.
And when I look at Mother Teresa's eyes,
I clearly see that her compassion-eyes
Can never be emptied.

Mother Teresa time and again tells us
That a smile from the heart
Knows no replacement.

In her blessingful presence,
It is not she, but we
Who gladly and instantly chop down
Our proud, giant mind-trees.

Mother Teresa always reminds us
That each difficulty
Is nothing short of God's Confidence
   In us.

With her Infinity's compassion-heart,
Mother Teresa is every day
Embracing countless, sorrowful hearts
Of forthcoming centuries.

GODS'S OWN AUTOGRAPH

Mother Teresa tells
Not only her suffering patients,
But also each and every human being,
'The answer to life is not self-doubt-imprisonment,
But self-discovery-enlightenment.
We are all God's children.'

The moment I think of Mother Teresa,
I immediately step forward in faith,
    God-faith.

Mother Teresa tells her dying patients
That God's Heart-Room
   Knows no closed doors.

Mother Teresa tells us
That if we want to succeed
   In the battlefield of life,
Then we must never separate
   Life from compassion.

GODS'S OWN AUTOGRAPH

The faith-bird in Mother Teresa
    Sings and dances
Long before it sees the clearing dawn.

What does she tell her patients?
    She tells them,
'Look, look, God is all ready to blossom
    In you!
He is His sleepless Thirst for you.'

Mother Teresa tells her patients
That God's Dream-Fulfilment
Is definitely attainable in and through them.

Mother Teresa lovingly and tenderly
    Advises us
Not to hesitate in accelerating
The manifestation of our heart-smiles.

Is there anybody on earth
Who will not see eye to eye with us
When we say that Mother Teresa
Is indeed God's special Way
To comfort the suffering and bleeding humanity?

Mother,
We claim to love
Your compassion-heart,
But you love to claim
Our affliction-lives.

O Absolute Lord Supreme,
You have made our Mother
The embodiment of compassion.
    Do make us
The embodiment of gratitude.

The moment I come
And stand in Mother Teresa's blessingful presence,
I see nothing but waves of smiles
Flowing from her compassion-flooded eyes.

GODS'S OWN AUTOGRAPH

Some pieces of advice
From Mother Teresa:
   Think of others first,
     Always;
  Let faith in the power of love
    Excel in your life;
  Remove all your self-destructive,
    Negative thoughts;
  Every minute do something
    To make all the children of God
    Happy and smiling.

Mother Teresa has numberless friends,
But her very best friend
　Is her heart's silence-prayer.

In her we see the revelation
　Of her Eternity's soul,
And the full manifestation
　Of her Divinity's heart.

Mother Teresa tells us
To do two things simultaneously:
   To touch God's Feet
     With our humility-mind;
   To feel God's Heart
     With our purity-life.

Mother Teresa tells us:
'Do not hesitate!
It is already too late.
   Put the Lord
In every corner of your life
Prayerfully and self-givingly.'

Sleeplessly and breathlessly,
With giant eagerness-strides,
Mother Teresa is paving the way
For a sickness and bitterness-free world.

Twenty-four hours a day
Mother Teresa lives inside
Her golden heart and silver tongue.

GODS'S OWN AUTOGRAPH

Mother Teresa shows us
How we can hold our sorrowful outer life
Up to our own inner light
By virtue of our sincere prayers.

Mother Teresa tells us
That in order to be truly happy
We must unreservedly feel our oneness-heart
With the breath of the poor.

Each and every poor life
   And sick body
Receives from Mother Teresa's heart
   A consolation-prize
And from her soul
   An illumination-surprise.

Mother Teresa reminds us
Of something extremely significant:
Power itself has no true power.
Power has power only when
Love-compassion-blossoms are found
   Inside it.

How profusely and immensely
Mother Teresa inspires us to see
   The God-aspiring, God-inspiring
And God-serving life-tree
Inside our own heart-garden!

The moment Mother Teresa
Approaches a poor, hungry heart,
God Himself spreads
A Compassion-Feast.

To our greatest delight,
Although Mother has seen 87 summers,
Fatigue does not dare to sit
On her sleepless enthusiasm.

Mother Teresa is not blind to
   The world's shortcomings,
But her forgiveness-heart
Is larger than the largest.
Therefore, she is able to house
All the world's shortcomings.

She has a special message for mankind:
Pray and pray and pray
For the fulfilment
   Of all your dreams.

She also tells us:
Life is not for complaining.
Life is for self-perfection.
Life is for God-satisfaction.

    It is true
That Heaven heals earth's sorrows.
    It is equally true
That a Heaven-born child
By the name of Teresa
Self-givingly heals earth's sorrows
    In boundless measure.

When you are in front of Mother Teresa,
Earthbound desires leave you
And Heaven-born desires enter into you.
These Heaven-born desires are:
    To feed the poor,
    To serve the needy.
Lo, you will see that
The redeemer and the sufferer
        Are none other
        Than Christ Himself.

Not only unique but unsurpassable
She will forever remain
In lighting the hope-candles of countless lives
With her heart's sun-faith-flames.

When we soulfully offer Mother
  What we have:
    A gratitude-heart,
She blesses us
  With what she is:
    Her Infinity's energy-life.

Every day Mother Teresa invites
True God-servers for the poor
   And the needy
To enjoy an ego-fat-free life,
   Which is the most delicious
      God-Bliss-diet.

When Mother Teresa bathes
The patients fast-approaching death
With her compassion-heart,
   Compassion-eyes and
      Compassion-hands,
Her soul and her Lord Jesus
Bathe in the sea of Infinity's Ecstasy.

GODS'S OWN AUTOGRAPH

Service, service, service!
Mother Teresa wants us to serve
God the creation
Sleeplessly and breathlessly,
And when we ask her
What will happen
If we serve God the way
She wants us to serve Him,
Mother tells us:
'Come and see me!
For you, I am the fastest escalator
To God's floor of Delight!'

She tells us to fight off
The waves of constant fear
While nursing the death-bound patients.
Lo, we become the beauty
　Of the Mother Earth;
We become the Fragrance
　Of Father Heaven.

The moment I imagine
　The Mother's Eternity's service-eyes,
I become the world-inspiration-starter.

The moment I feel
　Her Infinity's service-heart,
I become the world-champion-winner.

GODS'S OWN AUTOGRAPH

Mother Teresa's blessingful message
  To us is this:
The end is freedom from living and dying.
The end is eternal life.
Until then, patience.

Something more she tells us:
Forgive and forgive quickly.
Even slow forgiveness
  Is infinitely better
Than no forgiveness.

Finally, the most important message
   From Mother Teresa
Echoes and re-echoes in our aspiration-heart:
   God is constantly watching
Our love-devotion-surrender-watch.
Our heart responds to His Whispering,
Our life to His Beckoning.

A Cosmopolitan Heart

REFLECTIONS ON MOTHER TERESA'S
LIFE AND WORDS

"God Never Condemned People to Suffer"

O children of Mother India, Mother Teresa is right. She is always right. Please believe in what she says about God and the suffering of humanity. What she says is from her oneness with God through her sleepless prayers:

"It is very difficult to convince people in India that God never condemned people to suffer."

Called Upon to Be Faithful

For people who have lovingly and devotedly applied themselves to charity, for religious people and spiritual people, for self-giving people, what Mother Teresa says is supremely momentous:
"We are called upon not to be successful, but to be faithful."

The Supremely Choice Instrument of Our Lord

By saying the right thing and by doing the right thing, not only for the ordinary people but also for the world figures, Mother Teresa has become the right person—the supremely choice instrument of our Heavenly Lord Himself. But it is difficult, if not impossible, for us to follow in her footsteps. During the Gulf War, for example, Mother Teresa wrote to both President George Bush of the United States and to President Saddam Hussein of Iraq imploring them to desist from a war which was ruining millions of innocent lives.

A Cosmopolitan Heart

Who else is a cosmopolitan heart if not Mother Teresa? Who else if not Mother Teresa wants each and every human being, in accordance with his own religious beliefs, to be perfect in his own way by bringing down illumination from Above?

When people attack her with a volley of criticism that she is turning everybody to Christianity, her pure and dauntless self-defence runs, "I *do* convert. I convert you to be a better Hindu, a better Catholic, a better Muslim, Jain or Buddhist. I would like to help you find God. When you find Him, it is up to you what you want with Him."

Giving the House Back to God

Mother Teresa's self-giving heart is for all. Her sincerity-mind, purity-heart and divinity-life conquer all human souls, no matter who the individual is and no matter which faith he belongs to. Each and every faith she claims as her very own.

Whatever Mother Teresa expects from her prayer-life, God the Giver fulfils through some individuals; for her work is none other than God's Work itself. Once a Muslim magistrate from Calcutta was moving to Dhaka and selling his house. The Church wanted to buy the house for Mother Teresa's rapidly expanding Order. They offered him 125,000 rupees, which was too low. He told Mother Teresa he would make his decision shortly. Then he went to a nearby mosque to pray before deciding whether to accept the offer. When he returned, he said, with tears in his eyes, "I got that house from God. I give it back to Him."

His house is now the Motherhouse of Mother Teresa's Missionaries of Charity.

Leader of a Divine and Disciplined Army

Discipline in any sphere of life is of paramount importance. No discipline, no fulfilment. Mother Teresa's is the life of constant inner and outer discipline. This discipline-virtue she wants each and every individual to embody if one wants either inner progress or outer success or both.

An amazing, amusing and illumining incident let us share with the world. Mother Teresa's own affection-flooded brother, Lazar, was a military officer. He told a journalist his own words to his sister: "You are like me; you are an officer. You could have gone to military school." Then he added: "You could really say that she is the commander of a unit—indeed, of a whole army. She has incredible strength of will, as our mother had. She is a conscientious and disciplined Catholic. This discipline is something she has and so has her entire congregation. It is a very austere Order, organised down to the smallest detail, with very precise rules. And she is their leader."

Mother's Action Is Her Recommendation

Mother Teresa's action is her own recommendation. Once India's Prime Minister Jawaharlal Nehru accepted an invitation from her, but Nehru fell ill. In spite of his illness, Nehru came to her place. Mother wanted to tell him something about her work. Nehru's immediate reply was: "No, Mother, you need not tell me about your work. I know it. That is why I have come."

The Living Mother Kali

There was a time when Mother Teresa was victim to many complaints made by Hindus. They thought she would eventually convert everybody to her Christianity. They begged the Police Commissioner to come and inspect Nirmal Hriday, her home for the dying, which is located near the sacred Kali Temple in the Kalighat district. In response to the complaints, the Police Commissioner came to her Nirmal Hriday. When he saw the way she was treating the patients—so prayerfully, so soulfully and with such self-abnegation—he was deeply moved. He told these critics, "You see a black stone image of the goddess Kali in the temple, but here I have seen the living Kali!" Mother Teresa transformed the inspector into a truth-seer, truth-believer and truth-executor.

Not the Plenitude but the Attitude

Not the plenitude, but the attitude. Not the gift, but what embodies the gift. The heart-giver Mother Teresa values infinitely more than the mind-giver.

She tells us: "It was late in the day (around ten at night) when the doorbell rang. I opened the door and found a man shivering from the cold.

"'Mother Teresa, I heard that you just received an important prize. When I heard this, I decided to offer you something, too. Here—you have it: this is what I collected today.'

"It was little, but in his case it was everything. I was moved more than by the Nobel Prize."

"Are You Praying for Me?"

TREASURED MEETINGS, SELECTED
TELEPHONE CONVERSATIONS AND LETTERS

— FIRST MEETING —

On 24 October 1975 a Spiritual Summit Conference was held at the United Nations Headquarters in New York. It was sponsored by the Temple of Understanding. Sri Chinmoy led the opening meditation, in the presence of UN Secretary-General Kurt Waldheim, and presented a rose to each speaker. Ms. Eileen Egan, a co-worker of Mother Teresa and a close companion from 1955, describes this occasion in her authoritative work Such a Vision of the Street *(Doubleday & Co., 1985):*

"On Friday, October 24 (1975), Mother Teresa was on the dais of a hall adjoining the United Nations Headquarters in New York. Beside Mother Teresa on the dais were the Lord Abbot Kosho Ohtani, a representative of Buddhism; Rabbi Robert Gordis, speaking for Judaism; Dr. Seyyed Houssein Nasr, speaking for Islam; and Srimati Gayatri Devi, for Hinduism. Mother Teresa was the Christian speaker.

"The opening meditation by Sri Chinmoy, leader of the meditation group at the United Nations, turned out to be a time devoted to utter silence.

"Mother Teresa spoke on God's love, the heart of the message brought by Jesus. She asked the participants—Jews, Christians, Muslims, Hindus and Buddhists—to serve the poor and suffering as 'brothers and sisters in the same family, created by the same loving God.'"

"ONE IS THE HUMAN SPIRIT"

THE SPIRITUAL SUMMIT MEETING
CALLED BY THE TEMPLE of UNDERSTANDING TO MARK THE
30TH ANNIVERSARY OF THE UNITED NATIONS

FRIDAY, OCTOBER 24, 1975

UNITED NATIONS

OPENING MEDITATION
Sri Chinmoy, Leader, Peace Meditation at the United Nations

WELCOME BY
His Excellency Mr. Kurt Waldheim, Secretary-General, the United Nations

INTRODUCTON
Charles J. Mills, President, The Temple of Understanding

STATEMENT BY
RELIGIOUS NON-GOVERNMENTAL ORGANIZATIONS AT
UNITED NATIONS HEADQUARTERS

INTRODUCTION OF SPIRITUAL LEADERS
Dr. Ewert H. Cousins, Conference Coordinator

ADDRESSES
Srimata Gayatri Devi: HINDUISM
Lord Abbot Kosho Ohtani: BUDDHISM
Rabbi Robert Gordis: JUDAISM
Mother Teresa: CHRISTIANITY
Dr. Seyyed Hossein Nasr: ISLAM

**JOINT-STATEMENT OF SPIRITUAL LEADERS ATTENDING SPIRITUAL SUMMIT
CONFERENCE V**
read by
Dr. Jean Houston, Conference Chairman

CLOSING PRAYER
Brother David Steindl-Rast, O.S.B., Monk of Mount Savior Monastery

United Nations
24 October 1975

— LETTER FROM MOTHER TERESA —

July   1989

Dear Sri Chinmoy,

This brings you my prayer and best wishes on the occasion of the Silver Jubilee of your 25 years in the US.

Let us more and more allow God to use us as instruments of His peace through our willingness to love as He loves. May you make way for peace by encouraging all who approach you to love, to give and especially to forgive. Forgiveness of others by not judging their motives, by loving them until it hurts removes anger and all other hindrances to true peace. May you continue to realize peace in yourself through all you are and strive to be. God bless your efforts.

God bless you
M Teresa mc

— Second Meeting —

The following is an account of the meeting Sri Chinmoy had with Mother Teresa at the Missionaries of Charity House, adjoining the Church of San Gregorio, in Rome, Italy, on 1 October 1994.

It was four-thirty in the afternoon. I was waiting for Mother Teresa in a very small room, and about forty of my students were waiting outside the building. She came into the room and placed her hands on my head. She blessed me and said, "I am so happy you have come to see me. I have heard so many things about you, such good things. I am so happy, so happy."

Because this was her private room, I had placed my sandals in a corner and I was wearing only my socks. She noticed that I was not wearing sandals and she said, "Please do not mind that I am wearing my sandals. My feet are chilled." Then she said, "Since I am wearing sandals, you also must wear your sandals." I put on my sandals again and we both sat down. I gave her some flowers.

She explained that when she arrived at the airport from Albania at three o'clock, she was supposed to go to another meeting. But she cancelled it and came directly to see me.

Then I spoke a few words to her in Bengali, but she wanted to speak to me in English. She speaks Bengali fluently, but she did not want to use it.

We were sitting at a very small table. My hands were folded over my heart. After a few seconds, she reached out and pulled my left hand towards her. Then she started pressing my fingers, one by one, from the tip of the finger to the wrist. When she finished with my left hand, she took my right hand from my heart and did the same thing—examining it and pressing this finger and that finger with such affection. One moment she was acting like a mother, the next moment like an elder sister, and the third like a younger sister. It was like a brother and sister having a family gathering. No other world figure has shown me this kind of affection!

Then we both began to speak at once. I was telling her, "You are the Mother of compassion," and she was telling me, "You have great love. You are always doing something wonderful for God."

I replied, "Mother, you are doing it through us. We are only mere instruments."

She showed me pictures on her wall of the poor people and the lepers in Calcutta and of some of the children she has helped. She told me so proudly that the sari she was wearing was made by a leper. She said that she has given help to over 130,000 poor and needy people.

I said, "You have conquered their hearts. You have not only conquered them but you have conquered India; not only India but the entire world. The entire world has boundless gratitude to you. You have elevated the consciousness of the entire world. And, Mother, every day you are feeding thousands of people. You have opened 440 houses to feed the poor and out of those, 120 are in

"ARE YOU PRAYING FOR ME?"

India. I have read all about your constant sacrifice. You are the Mother of constant sacrifice."

She replied, "Jesus Christ suffered so much for the love of us. I feel that this is our way of sharing His suffering. He said something so beautiful: 'Whatever you do to the least of My brethren, you do to Me.' It is Him we serve in the poor and the sick. They are poorer than the poorest; they have all kinds of diseases, but God loves them. Jesus said, 'For I was hungry and you gave Me food, I was thirsty and you gave Me drink, naked and you clothed Me, sick and you cared for Me and helped Me.'"

While she was speaking, I could see that her whole being was flooded with compassion. I said to her, "Mother, your compassion is saving the world."

"There are many, many people involved," she said.

"We belong to one family," I added. Then Mother Teresa began to narrate many stories about her life. Some of them were very private and personal experiences which must remain confidential; other incidents I had read in books about her life. How she opened her heart to me!

She said, "A young couple came to my House to get my blessings and they gave me 10,000 rupees. Such a large amount of money! I asked them, 'How did you get it?' They said that they had just been married. They did not buy wedding clothes and they did not have a wedding party because they had decided to come and give all the money to me to use for the poor. When I asked them why they had made this sacrifice, they said: 'We wanted to share the joy of loving.' Can you imagine! Ten thousand rupees they gave me."

Then I said, "You did not mention the figure, 10,000 rupees, in your book."

"Yes," she said, "it was 10,000 that they gave me."

"Mother, I also have something for you," I said. In my pocket I had an envelope with a little money inside as an offering to her. I felt that it was the golden opportunity to give it. With all my heart I gave her my love-offering. As usual, I had drawn birds on the envelope when I sealed it. In this case, there were three birds. Mother Teresa liked them so much. She was pressing the envelope and looking at me with such affectionate tenderness.

I was reminded of another story I had read about her. I said, "Children love you so much. One little four-year-old boy found out that you did not have any sugar. So he did not take sugar for three days. Then he came with his parents and gave you the small amount of sugar that he had saved.

"Another little boy did not want to have his birthday party at home. He wanted to have it at your place, with all the poor children.

"One rich lady came to you. She always bought her saris for 800 rupees. You asked her to buy them for 500 rupees and give the rest to the poor. Then gradually she brought it down to 300 rupees and even 100 rupees. When she was buying saris for 100 rupees, you told her: 'Do not go lower than this.' "

"ARE YOU PRAYING FOR ME?"

These stories about the love people have for Mother Teresa are so moving. I was telling some details which I had read and she was adding more. At one point, I mentioned the happiest day in her life—when the present Pope came to Calcutta and visited Nirmal Hriday. Mother Teresa told me that on that day she was praying and praying to God for only one thing: that somebody should die in front of the Pope. She wanted the Pope to see a man die. And God answered her prayers.

Then Mother Teresa asked me, "Where are you from?"

"I am a Bengali. I come from Bangladesh and I was born in Chittagong," I replied. Then I said Chittagong in our own dialect—Chatragram.

"We have a house in Dhaka," said Mother Teresa. "Over 1,000 children have come there."

"Children come to their real mother," I said. "You are their real mother. I shall always remember Prime Minister Nehru's immortal utterance when he visited Shishu Bhavan, your children's home in Delhi. He told you, 'Take special care of these children. One of them might be Prime Minister one day.'"

When Mother Teresa speaks, she is so full of life. Sometimes she would point her finger at me and, again, how many times she just clasped my hands and held them! It is exactly like sisterly or motherly affection.

At this point in our conversation, I became inspired to introduce President Gorbachev's name. I said, "President Gorbachev has such admiration for you. He is a very close friend of mine. When he

MEETINGS, CONVERSATIONS AND LETTERS

heard that I was coming here for your blessings, he and his wife, Raisa Maximovna, and also all those who work at the Gorbachev Foundation, asked me to offer you their most soulful prayers and devotion. They are sending you their utmost gratitude. Do you know President Gorbachev?"

"His name is Mikhail but I say Michael," she answered. "I have not met him, but every year on the Feast Day of Saint Michael I remember him and send him a letter. But he never corresponds with me."

"He is so grateful to you because you went to Armenia when the earthquake took place," I said.

Mother Teresa then told me that she was very eager to meet with President Gorbachev.

I went on, "I am so grateful to you, Mother. Today my life is being blessed. For the last twenty years I have been trying to have your darshan."

Mother Teresa asked me, "Where do you live?"

"I live in America, in New York," I replied. "For thirty years I have been there. Every Tuesday and Friday I offer prayers at the United Nations. It began with U Thant. Many years ago, you came to the United Nations. About twenty religious leaders came. I offered you a rose, Mother, and you gave a talk."

Mother Teresa said, "U Thant had passed away by the time I came to the United Nations for that religious programme, so I could not meet him."

"True," I said, "he has passed away, but he is with us in spirit. He was a true man of peace and, in honour of him, every year I offer the U Thant Peace Award. The Executive Director of UNICEF, Mr. James Grant, has received this award recently. I would like to offer it to you now with my deepest devotion. I have written a song for you which I would like my students to sing for you."

As Mother Teresa and I made our way to the courtyard outside, she said, "Do you know how many people we have picked up from the streets of Calcutta since I began my work in 1952? 65,000. And Hindus, Christians and Muslims have all died side by side. They are real children of God. Not one has died distressed."

I said, "You have made them feel, Mother, that they are children of God. They did not know what they were here on earth for, but you have made them feel that they are chosen children of God."

"I have never heard a word of complaint from our sick and dying," said Mother Teresa. "They die of hunger, disease of the blood, cancer—but they never complain. I have heard many rich people complain, but never those who come to us."

"That is because you have brought forward the divinity of Jesus Christ from within them," I said.

Mother Teresa continued, "Jesus has made it very clear to me: 'Give to the least.' When we die and go to God, again we will see God's Face. Here on earth we must serve Him in the poor and the sick. And we must save the children. 'I was poor and you gave Me.' Those are His words. That is why our work is so beautiful."

"Your work is beautiful because you are beautiful," I said. "Your heart is a flower and they are getting the fragrance of the flower."

With utmost humility, Mother Teresa said, "God has given me many sisters to help me in my work. We have more than one thousand. In such a short time we have gone up, up, up. And there is so much love between the mother and the sisters."

We were now standing outside in the courtyard. Just an hour before our meeting it had been pouring with rain but now, by some miracle, it had stopped. I asked the singers to sing two songs which I had composed for Mother Teresa: "Compassion-Mother" and "Nirmal Hriday." She was following the printed music with her finger and enjoying it immensely. At the end, she said, "Beautiful, beautiful. Thank you very much." Then we began our presentation of the U Thant Peace Award.

MR. ADHIRATHA KEEFE: This symbolic presentation by members of Sri Chinmoy: The Peace Meditation at the United Nations is to Mother Teresa, Compassion-Heart and Service-Life of India, whose loving tears and blessingful touch have assuaged the agonies of countless human lives and whose devotedly, radiantly and unreservedly self-giving example has kindled the flame of self-dedication of world-serving brothers and sisters everywhere. (*Reads the inscription on the plaque*) Mother Teresa: Nobel Peace Laureate of sacred humility, prayerful server of Divinity, soulful lover of humanity. From Sri Chinmoy: The Peace Meditation at the United Nations. October 1st, 1994."

"ARE YOU PRAYING FOR ME?"

Mother Teresa receives the plaque.

MOTHER TERESA: Thank you, thank you. I have heard so much about your work all over the world. I am so pleased with what you are doing for people in so many countries. May God bless you, Sri Chinmoy, and all your wonderful work for peace. May we continue to work together and to share together, all for the glory of God and for the good of man.

MR. SHAMBHU VINEBERG: Mother, every two years Sri Chinmoy sponsors a run for world peace in over seventy countries around the world. This torch has been held by the Holy Father. *(Sri Chinmoy hands the Peace Torch to Mother Teresa.)*

MOTHER TERESA: Now Mother is holding the Peace Torch! *(Turning to Sri Chinmoy)* You should hold it, too.

Mother Teresa and Sri Chinmoy hold the torch together. Sri Chinmoy then presents Mother Teresa with the "Lifting Up the World with a Oneness-Heart" medallion. This medallion has been presented to eminent people from all walks of life whose works have helped to lift up the standard of humanity.

MOTHER TERESA: Thank you very much and God bless you in whatever you do for God. It is not how much we do but how much love we have in our hearts that is important. Remember, words of love are words of peace. By praying together, you will also find love. Families that pray together, stay together. And if you stay together, you will love each other as God loves each one of you.

Jesus Christ came to give us the good news that God loves us and that He wants us to love one another as He loves each one of us. And to make it easier for us to love one another, He says, 'Whatever you do for the least, you do for Me.' And at the end of our life, when we die and go Home to God, He will say, 'Come, enter into Heaven. Because I was hungry, you gave Me food; I was naked and you clothed Me; I was homeless and you sheltered Me; I was sick and you cared for Me; I was in prison and you visited Me.' This is what you are all trying to do, this is how you will be able to keep the joy of loving God in your hearts. Just take somebody; just love somebody; just give peace and joy to somebody to thank God for His great Love. Thank God for all the beautiful things.

SRI CHINMOY *(to his students)*: Please bring the medicine.

MOTHER TERESA: Gather the medicine and I will take it to Calcutta. You must come to Calcutta one day.

Sri Chinmoy's students place two large boxes of medicine on the ground in front of Mother Teresa. The supplies had been brought from America to help her in her work.

"ARE YOU PRAYING FOR ME?"

MOTHER TERESA: I thank you on behalf of the poor. You have given a very precious gift for all, a most beautiful gift.

Mother Teresa then requests one of her Sisters to bring her "business cards." Sri Chinmoy's students walk past Mother Teresa and she hands each one a card. Her "business card" is actually a small card with one of her prayers printed on it and her name. As each person walks by, Sri Chinmoy tells her that individual's nationality. He explains that over 700 of his students have come to Rome.

MOTHER TERESA: This card will remind you of God, to pray for me and all our Brothers and Sisters that we may all continue God's Work with great love.

Sri Chinmoy notices that the prayer on the card is the same one that he has recently set to music.

SRI CHINMOY: Mother, may I take one more minute from you? This particular prayer I have set tune to. I was so moved by these words that I set them to music.

The singers sing the song. The prayer is:

> The fruit of silence is prayer.
> The fruit of prayer is faith.
> The fruit of faith is love.
> The fruit of love is service.
> The fruit of service is peace.
> — *Mother Teresa*

MOTHER TERESA *(to the singers)*: You should come to Calcutta and work with the dying. There are 70 young people like you from all over the world. They come and pray early in the morning and work the whole day with the dying, the sick and the lepers. Then, in the evening, we all pray together again. They are beautiful volunteers. So when you are going around the world, stop in Calcutta!

Mother Teresa then leads her Sisters in a prayer of thanks.

MOTHER TERESA: These are my very special prayers. When we pray together, you will be in our prayers. We will say this special prayer for you for God's Blessings.

And I am so happy to receive special medicine for the lepers.

We have now treated almost 7,000 cases of leprosy in India. The government is very good to me. They give me land to use for rehabilitating them. I pay only one rupee a year and that makes me the owner. I do not pay taxes and this kind of thing. The Indian Government does so much, so much.

We give each husband and wife a little house of their own. They stay together and nobody runs away, thank God.

Now we have opened places to do God's Work in Russia and in Viet Nam. In Viet Nam there are so many crippled children and we are starting to work with them. So pray for us to do God's Work with great love. God bless you all, thank you, thank you so much. Pray for us.

And whenever you visit Calcutta, remember my business card! One day a man came to me and said, "Mother, do you have a business card?" I said, "I am sorry. I do not have a business card." On his way out, he said, "Give me something with one of your prayers on it." Then after three days, he came back and said, "I have made these business cards for you." That is why we call it a business card.

Pray for us that we do not spoil life and that we can continue doing God's Work with great love. And I especially want you to pray that we can open a place for AIDS. In the United States and Europe there are a great number of cases, so pray for us that people can die at peace with God. Up to now, we have not been able to find a cure, but if we all pray, I feel perhaps God will give us a cure. Thank you, God bless you, thank you, thank you.

* * * * * *

Sri Chinmoy's closing remarks:

And so my happy, happier, happiest meeting with Mother Teresa came to an end after forty-five minutes. Right from the beginning of our private interview, Mother Teresa showed me so many signs of affection, kindness and respect. I was so deeply moved by her love and compassion for the suffering humanity.

Mother Teresa lovingly blesses Sri Chinmoy, and he devotedly offers his homage to her and prayers for her. They speak privately at the start of their first interview on 1 October 1994. The meeting was held at the Missionaries of Charity House in Rome, adjoining the San Gregorio Church, and lasted forty-five minutes.

Mother shares with Sri Chinmoy many deeply inspiring, soul-stirring stories from her sleepless service-life.

Outside in the courtyard for the second part of their meeting, Sri Chinmoy shows Mother the songs that he has composed about her both in English and in Bengali. Bengali is his native tongue and it is Mother Teresa's adopted tongue.

Sri Chinmoy's students from many countries sing for Mother Teresa, as she prayerfully follows the music with her finger.

A member of the Peace Meditation group reads out the inscription on the U Thant Peace Award to Mother Teresa. He gratefully cites her limitless compassion-heart and her sleepless service-life.

Sri Chinmoy bows to Mother Teresa after presenting her with the U Thant Peace Award on behalf of the Peace Meditation at the United Nations. In 1970, at the invitation of then Secretary-General U Thant, Sri Chinmoy began leading twice-weekly Peace Meditations at the United Nations for delegates and staff. The U Thant Peace Award is presented to individuals who, in exemplifying the lofty spiritual ideals of the late Secretary-General, have offered distinguished service toward the attainment of world peace. Other recipients include President Mikhail Gorbachev, President Nelson Mandela and Archbishop Desmond Tutu.

The U Thant Peace Award. The citation reads:
>The U Thant Peace Award is presented to Mother Teresa, Compassion-Heart and Service-Life of India, whose loving tears and blessingful touch have assuaged the agonies of countless human lives, and whose devotedly, radiantly and unreservedly self-giving example has kindled the flame of self-dedication in world-serving brothers and sisters everywhere.
>
>Mother Teresa: Nobel Peace Laureate of sacred humility, prayerful server of divinity, soulful lover of humanity.

> *"The simplicity and humility that prevails in the Missionaries of Charity constitutions is very clear and its spirit may be used as so many have done and are doing. Not to us, O Lord, not to us but to Your Name be glory!"* — MOTHER TERESA

Sri Chinmoy proudly and happily offers the Peace Torch from the worldwide, 70-nation Sri Chinmoy Oneness-Home Peace Run to Mother Teresa.

Holding the Peace Torch aloft with matchless enthusiasm, Mother offers unimaginable joy to all present.

"May we continue to work together and to share together, all for the glory of God and for the good of man."
MOTHER TERESA

Mother Teresa and Sri Chinmoy share precious moments filled with spiritual joy during their interview.

Mother Teresa lovingly blesses one of Sri Chinmoy's students who had devotedly coordinated the collection of many boxes of medical supplies which were offered to Mother Teresa.

Mother showers her compassionate affection on one of Sri Chinmoy's students who had earlier spoken with her by telephone in preparation for the meeting.

— TELEPHONE CONVERSATION —

15 October 1994

SRI CHINMOY: Mother, this is Sri Chinmoy. How are you feeling today?

MOTHER TERESA: I am just fine. I am sure you are praying for me.

SRI CHINMOY: Yes, Mother! Every day I am praying for you with all my heart and soul. Tomorrow I shall be meeting with President Gorbachev. Do you have any message you would like me to offer to him?

MOTHER TERESA: I am so happy that you will be meeting with him. Please tell him that we have 15 houses in Russia. I would like to meet him, but he is so busy!

SRI CHINMOY: I shall definitely offer him your message. Mother, I do hope to see you again soon.

MOTHER TERESA: Definitely we shall be together! God bless you.

NOTE: The telephone conversations between Sri Chinmoy and Mother Teresa truly spanned the globe. While he usually called her from his home in New York, Mother Teresa was to be found in Calcutta or visiting her Houses in various parts of the world.

— TELEPHONE CONVERSATION —

18 October 1994

Sri Chinmoy informed Mrs. Irina Malikova, Deputy Director of International Relations and Media of the Gorbachev Foundation, that Mother Teresa mentioned she writes to President Gorbachev every year, but he does not respond, and also that she would like to meet with him. Mrs. Malikova conveyed Mother's message to President Gorbachev.

* * * * *

After a few weeks Mrs. Malikova informed Sri Chinmoy that President Gorbachev had already sent his Christmas card to Mother. Sri Chinmoy happily and proudly shared the good news with Mother on the telephone.

— TELEPHONE CONVERSATION —

23 November 1994

SRI CHINMOY: Mother, I wish to offer you a small piece of happy news. By God's Grace I have been able to complete 700 peace-poems. Each poem is my heartfelt prayer for world peace.

MOTHER TERESA: Wonderful! Thank God! Sri Chinmoy, together we will work and together we will pray for peace. This will bring many people to God. Works of peace are works of love and works of love are works of peace. Please keep praying that we continue doing God's Work.

SRI CHINMOY: Thank you, Mother, for your blessingful and illumining words. I shall continue praying every day for you from the very depths of my aspiration-heart.

MOTHER TERESA: By the way, I have received a Christmas card from President Gorbachev. His greeting card has come first before anybody else's card!

"ARE YOU PRAYING FOR ME?"

SRI CHINMOY: Mother, I am so happy. I am so happy. During our last interview you told me that he never writes to you. I informed him. Mother, he is a really good man with a big heart.

MOTHER TERESA: I know that. Now you and I must continue praying for each other. May God bless you!

Following their telephone conversation, Sri Chinmoy informed Mrs. Irina Malikova that President Gorbachev's Christmas card had arrived first. She informed President Gorbachev and he was very pleased.

— TELEPHONE CONVERSATION —

6 February 1995

A STUDENT OF SRI CHINMOY'S: Mother, Sri Chinmoy has asked me to convey his prayerful love and gratitude to you.

MOTHER TERESA: How is Sri Chinmoy? Thank God! Thank God!

STUDENT: Sri Chinmoy has recently been in Viet Nam and offered many wonderful programmes for peace.

MOTHER TERESA: Very good! Very good! We have opened houses there. I am going again. Please ask Sri Chinmoy to pray for us. I will write to Sri Chinmoy! Please send me his address once more. Yes! Sri Chinmoy is working so hard for peace all over the world!

STUDENT: Mother, Sri Chinmoy would like to know if you have received the letter from President Gorbachev inviting you to become a member of the International Gorbachev Trust for Children's Health Care.

"ARE YOU PRAYING FOR ME?"

MOTHER TERESA: No, it has not yet come. Let the letter come and then we can speak again. I am very anxious to get President Gorbachev's letter! We have 13 houses in Russia!

How God is sending people to us! The other day we had no milk to feed our 150 babies! A Hindu gentleman came. He heard a voice inside him telling him, "Go and bring milk to Mother Teresa!" And so he brought a big box. I opened the box to see and there was exactly enough milk for our babies! This is a living miracle! From early morning people are coming.

The other day I got a letter from a child in the United States. He said, "Mother Teresa, I love you so much. I am sending you my pocket money. Here is a check for three dollars."

One young man and woman just got married in India. They are both Hindus. They gave us 10,000 rupees. I couldn't believe it! Before their marriage they decided not to buy wedding clothes and to put the money aside for the poor. Not even a fancy sari or anything!

This is all God's Work! It is He, and not we, who is doing everything!

Tell Sri Chinmoy that he is in my very special prayers and ask him to pray for me.

— TELEPHONE CONVERSATION —

17 February 1995

SRI CHINMOY: Mother, I am calling for your blessings.

MOTHER TERESA: Pray for me.

SRI CHINMOY: Have you read President Gorbachev's letter?

MOTHER TERESA: I have not yet received it. Let us wait for his letter to come. One day you must come here to Calcutta to visit me!

SRI CHINMOY: I shall be very happy to come and visit you. In the meantime, I am praying for you every day.

MOTHER TERESA: Thank you! That is what we need the most.

— TELEPHONE CONVERSATION —

22 February 1995

SRI CHINMOY: Mother, I am calling you from New York. How are you feeling, Mother?

MOTHER TERESA: I am fine. Are you praying for me?

SRI CHINMOY: Definitely I am praying for you.

MOTHER TERESA: By the way, today I received the letter from President Gorbachev himself. I will pray over it and read it all, and tomorrow I will decide. Please call me tomorrow if you can.

SRI CHINMOY: Thank you, Mother. I shall definitely call you tomorrow.

— TELEPHONE CONVERSATION —

23 February 1995

SRI CHINMOY: Mother, I am praying for your blessings. What is your decision about President Gorbachev's letter?

MOTHER TERESA: I have decided. I do not mix with politics.

SRI CHINMOY: Mother, I tell you, he is an excellent man. I know him personally. Although he is a politician, he has done so much towards world peace for the betterment of the entire world. His life is all sacrifice. He united the two Germanys and he liberated countless millions of people in Hungary, Poland and Czechoslovakia. He is really a man of heart. I admire him like anything.

MOTHER TERESA: You do?

SRI CHINMOY: Yes, Mother, I do admire him and adore him. Mother, he has also asked me to join as an honorary member. He would like both of us to offer our prayers for him and for his service to the poor and sick children. I have very happily and proudly accepted, Mother.

"ARE YOU PRAYING FOR ME?"

MOTHER TERESA: Oh, very good! You are also praying! Yes, I can do that! I can pray for him and for the Russian children. In that case, I will gladly accept. I will write to President Gorbachev to tell him that I am accepting.

SRI CHINMOY: Mother, I know that President Gorbachev will be extremely happy and extremely grateful to you. For he knows that your sacred prayers will unmistakably be answered for his suffering Russian children. I am so proud and so honoured that he has also asked me to join with you, Mother, with my humble prayers.

MOTHER TERESA: God bless you! Please pray for me and for all our Sisters.

SRI CHINMOY: Yes, Mother, every day I pray for you with all my heart's love, devotion and gratitude.

— Letter from Mother Teresa —

+LDM   12th May, 1995.

Dear Sri Chinmoy,

        I congratulate you on your 31st anniversary of coming to America and serving humanity all over the world.

        I thank God for His love for you and for the joy with which you have served Him and continue serving Him. May He always be in you so that you grow more and more to be His love and compassion in the world.

        It is wonderful to think of God's great love for you and me - to give us the opportunity to do something beautiful for Him. My prayer for you and the group will be with you.

God bless you
M Teresa

— LETTER FROM MOTHER TERESA —

+LDM

MISSIONARIES OF CHARITY
54/A, A. J. C. Bose Road,
Calcutta - 700016 India

Dear Sri Chinmoy,

Thank you very much for your prayers and good wishes for me. Health or sickness all are God's gifts. Let us pray that we give God a free hand to use us without consulting us.

Keep the joy of loving God in your heart as your strength, and share this joy with all you come in touch with.

God bless you.

Mc Teresa m.

— LETTER FROM MOTHER TERESA —

+LDM   Dec. 1995

Dear Sri Chinmoy,

Thank you for your letter and for sharing in our works of love amongst the poorest of the poor through your gift.

Today God loves the world so much that He gives Himself. He gives YOU and me to be His love and compassion.

I take this opportunity to wish you a very Happy and Holy Birthday. May each one of us allow God to use as His instruments to bring peace in this world.

My prayer for you is my gift to you.

God bless you
M Teresa mc

— THIRD MEETING —

The following is a transcript of the meeting Sri Chinmoy had with Mother Teresa at the Missionaries of Charity House in the Bronx, New York City, on 4 June 1996.

MOTHER TERESA *(receiving Sri Chinmoy affectionately)*: I am so happy to see you, Sri Chinmoy, after such a long time!

SRI CHINMOY: Once more I have come to receive blessings from you, Mother.

MOTHER TERESA: God bless you! Thank you! God bless you! Thank you! *(Reciting her special prayer)* "The fruit of silence is prayer. The fruit of prayer is faith. The fruit of faith is love. The fruit of love is service. The fruit of service is peace." This is the prayer I recite every day.

SRI CHINMOY: Every day, Mother, I pray for your good health.

MOTHER TERESA: Thank you.

SRI CHINMOY: I have been living here in New York for the last 31 years. And I understand you came here 25 years ago. Your assistant was telling me that 25 years ago you came here.

MOTHER TERESA: Yes, in 1971 we started our Mission here.

SRI CHINMOY: I shall always remember our first meeting in 1975. There was a conference at the United Nations. Religious leaders came, and you very graciously blessed me in the Dag Hammarskjöld Auditorium. You came, Mother, along with other religious leaders, and at that time you blessed me.

MOTHER TERESA: You do so much for us.

SRI CHINMOY *(offering a donation)*: Mother, here is my offering to you, my small offering.

MOTHER TERESA *(with emphasis)*: Thank you.

SRI CHINMOY: Mother, it is my wish to honour you at the United Nations in the near future. You come to the United Nations from time to time. On the occasion of the Holy Father's birthday, I offered our prayers for him at the United Nations. Also, my students went to 76 churches and prayed for him, prayed for his good health, in honour of his birthday. So the same thing I would like to do for you at the United Nations. I would like to offer you our prayers.

MOTHER TERESA: I am too small for that.

SRI CHINMOY: No, you are not! Mother is always filled with Mother's affection.

MOTHER TERESA: Please pray for me.

SRI CHINMOY: And Mother, you promised me that you would not retire. As long as God keeps you physically on earth, I do not want you to retire.

MOTHER TERESA: I am not going to retire. I want to do God's Will.

SRI CHINMOY: Right! God's Will is for you to continue, not to retire. Sometimes you say that you are going to retire. That breaks our heart. You are the ocean of compassion for all those who come to you.

MOTHER TERESA: That is the beauty of running this congregation: everybody can accept and do God's Work beautifully together.

SRI CHINMOY: Yes, everybody together, but again there is a leader, and you are the supreme leader.

MOTHER TERESA: I am not the supreme leader. I am a mere instrument of the Lord.

SRI CHINMOY: You are the supremely chosen instrument.

MOTHER TERESA: Please pray for us.

SRI CHINMOY: Now my students would like to sing two songs about the Saviour Jesus Christ, and one short song about you.

The singers sing a song that Sri Chinmoy has set to the words of the Saviour Christ: "Not my will, but Thine be done" and "Father, forgive them, for they know not what they do." Then they perform Mother Teresa's own prayer that Sri Chinmoy had set to music: "The fruit of silence is prayer. The fruit of prayer is faith. The fruit of faith is love. The fruit of love is service. The fruit of service is peace."

SRI CHINMOY: Mother, these are your words. The gift of love—that is what you give us, Mother. Your love transforms clay into gold and coal into diamond.

"ARE YOU PRAYING FOR ME?"

MOTHER TERESA: When are you coming to Calcutta? Please keep my photo here, so that you can pray for me.

SRI CHINMOY: I am praying, definitely I am praying for you, Mother. Mother, I am so proud of you. Yesterday you received the "Courage of Conscience" award.

MOTHER TERESA: What a name, a beautiful name!

SRI CHINMOY: I am so proud of you, so proud of you. You deserve it! I am so happy.

Mother Teresa thanks Sri Chinmoy and affectionately says good-bye.

Mother Teresa lovingly welcomes Sri Chinmoy to her Missionaries of Charity House in the Bronx, New York on 4 June 1996.

Sri Chinmoy prays most soulfully and most powerfully with Mother Teresa as his students sing prayerful songs which Sri Chinmoy has set to music. The words are from the immortal utterances of the Saviour Christ, as well as Mother's prayer, "The fruit of silence is prayer..."

During their meeting, Mother shares with Sri Chinmoy her work of love in serving the needy and the unwanted in all parts of the world. She enthusiastically invites Sri Chinmoy to visit Calcutta and lovingly entreats his prayers.

Sri Chinmoy points out the "Courage of Conscience" award which Mother Teresa had recently received and offers to her his boundless pride and joy for this latest, most appropriate recognition.

— TELEPHONE CONVERSATION —

13 April 1997
4:45 a.m. New York time

SRI CHINMOY: I am calling from New York for your blessings, Mother. How are you feeling?

MOTHER TERESA: I am much better, thank God! Are you still praying for me?

SRI CHINMOY: Every day I pray for you. Mother, I have a piece of good news for you. In a few hours I shall be meeting with President Gorbachev. May I tell him that you are sending your blessings?

MOTHER TERESA: No, no. I can only pray for him. He is too great! Tell him that I shall pray for him.

SRI CHINMOY: Mother, soon I would like to call you again.

MOTHER TERESA: Do call. Pray for me. God bless you! Remember me always in your prayers.

"ARE YOU PRAYING FOR ME?"

SRI CHINMOY: Thank you, Mother. You are always and always in my prayers, Mother.

NOTE: This day holds a deep personal significance for Sri Chinmoy because it was on 13 April 1964 that he first arrived in New York from his native India.

Conversation with President Gorbachev about Mother Teresa

13 April 1997
11:00 a.m. New York time

Several hours after his telephone conversation with Mother Teresa, Sri Chinmoy had a private meeting with President Gorbachev and his wife, Raisa Maximovna, during their brief visit to New York. During the course of their discussion, Sri Chinmoy mentioned his earlier telephone conversation with Mother Teresa.

SRI CHINMOY *(looking at Raisa Maximovna)*: I am a man of prayer. Just this morning something very important happened. I spoke to Mother Teresa on the telephone. Mother Teresa told me she thinks of President Gorbachev, how great he is.

PRESIDENT GORBACHEV: How is she feeling?

SRI CHINMOY: She is much better. She will come to New York next month. I speak to her from time to time and she writes to me. So today I said to her, "In a few hours' time I shall meet with President Gorbachev. Would you like to offer him your blessings?"

"ARE YOU PRAYING FOR ME?"

She said, "He is such a great man! I am praying to God to bless him. But I cannot bless him, he is so great."

PRESIDENT GORBACHEV *(putting his hand on his head)*: She can! Because Gorbachev does not think in this way about himself. He considers himself to be a normal person.

SRI CHINMOY: But *she* thinks this way.

PRESIDENT GORBACHEV: Please, could you give her from myself and Raisa Maximovna the warmest feelings of support and our wishes for her good health.

RAISA MAXIMOVNA: And our deepest respects.

SRI CHINMOY: I shall tell her. Last time I met with her she told me that four years ago she had sent you a Christmas card. Last year, to her surprise and delight, she received her first Christmas card from you.

PRESIDENT GORBACHEV: I wanted to invite her to Milan for a conference of Nobel Prize laureates. But I was told later that she is ill and lying down.

SRI CHINMOY: Today, when I spoke to her, she seemed much better. She will come next month to New York.

PRESIDENT GORBACHEV: Good, very good.

RAISA MAXIMOVNA: It is wonderful to hear, Sri Chinmoy, that Mother Teresa is feeling better. I really admire her.

PRESIDENT GORBACHEV: Maybe we will be lucky enough to see her one day.

SRI CHINMOY: She will also be very lucky to meet with you!

PRESIDENT GORBACHEV: I really wanted her to go to Italy and meet with Nobel Prize laureates, so that they would give a message to the world which is now on the border of the twentieth and twenty-first centuries—because the world is again full of danger and anxiety.

Sri Chinmoy meets with President Mikhail Gorbachev and his wife, Raisa Maximovna, on 13 April 1997. The meeting took place on the same day as Sri Chinmoy's early morning telephone conversation with Mother Teresa. Sri Chinmoy proudly and happily conveyed Mother Teresa's sincere prayers for President Gorbachev.

SRI CHINMOY: THE PEACE MEDITATION AT THE UNITED NATIONS

UNITED NATIONS:

the Heart-Home
of the World-Body

We believe and we hold that each man has the potentiality of reaching the Ultimate Truth. We also believe that man cannot and will not remain imperfect forever. Each man is an instrument of God. When the hour strikes, each individual soul listens to the inner dictates of God. When man listens to God, his imperfections are turned into perfections, his ignorance into knowledge, his searching mind into revealing light and his uncertain reality into all-fulfilling Divinity.

April 16th, 1997

Mother Teresa
Missionaries of Charity
54A Acharya Jagadish Chandra Bose Rd.
Calcutta INDIA 700016

Dearest Mother,

    I am extremely grateful to you that you spoke with me and offered me your most sacred blessings a few days ago. I am so proud and happy that you will be coming to New York soon. Wherever you travel, countless aspiring souls have the unparalleled opportunity to be nourished by Mother's infinite love, affection and compassion. And these divine benedictions come directly from our Saviour Lord Himself. For this reason, it gives me tremendous joy to send you my love-offering to pay for your plane fare from India to New York.

    Mother, I wish to share with you that just a few hours after we spoke last Sunday, I met with President Mikhail Gorbachev and his wife Raisa Maximovna. I told the President that you are offering your special prayers for him, and he was so very happy. He told me that he is very eager to meet with you.

    I am praying to our Lord Supreme to grant You his choicest Blessings of Health and Joy so that you may continue to spread His Love-Light throughout the length and breadth of the entire world.

                Yours in the Supreme,

                 Sri Chinmoy

Sri Chinmoy: The Peace Meditation at the United Nations is an association of United Nations delegates, staff, NGO representatives and accredited press correspondents holding twice-weekly peace meditations and other programmes at United Nations Headquarters.

―LETTER FROM MOTHER TERESA―

+LDM   April, 1997

Dear Sri Chinmoy,

    Charity begins today. Today somebody is suffering, today somebody is in the street, today somebody is hungry. Our work is for today, yesterday has gone, tomorrow has not yet come. We have only today to make God - known, loved, served, fed, clothed, sheltered. Do not wait for tomorrow. Tomorrow we will not have them if we do not feed them today.

    Thank you for your gift through which you make this a reality in your lives.

    My gratitude is my prayer for you.

                   GOD BLESS YOU,

M Teresa mc

— FOURTH MEETING —

Mother Teresa invited Sri Chinmoy to visit her on the afternoon of 3 June 1997 at the Missionaries of Charity House in the Bronx, New York. When Sri Chinmoy arrives, Sister Sabita, Regional Superior of the Missionaries of Charity for the East Coast of the USA, opens the door and says that the Sisters have been expecting him. She is full of smiles and kindness.

They go inside, into the same small room where Sri Chinmoy had met Mother Teresa the year before, and Sister Paula-Marie greets him with a broad smile.

SISTER NIRMALA (*entering and introducing herself in a sweeter than the sweetest way, full of joy*): Sri Chinmoy, I am Nirmala. (*Sister Nirmala had been recently elected as Superior General of the Missionaries of Charity, the highest position.*)

SRI CHINMOY: Sister Nirmala! Congratulations, congratulations!

While congratulating her, Sri Chinmoy presents Sister Nirmala with a special gift to mark the occasion. This soulful gift is a mirror with Mother Teresa's picture engraved on it. The picture is surrounded by about 20 birds.

SISTER NIRMALA: Who drew these birds?

SRI CHINMOY: These are my birds.

Sister Nirmala is so happy and thrilled with the gift.

SRI CHINMOY *(to Sister Paula-Marie)*: Last time I was here, there was a very special award on the table.

Sister Paula-Marie opens up a cabinet and shows Sri Chinmoy an article in a magazine which has a picture of Mother Teresa receiving that particular award, the "Courage of Conscience" award.

Sister Nirmala comes back into the room, showing love and concern, just before Mother Teresa enters.

At 7:17 p.m. Mother Teresa enters through the side door, folding her hands. A young Sister helps Mother Teresa with the wheelchair that she is forced to use from time to time.

SRI CHINMOY *(with great joy)*: Mother, Mother, I have come for your blessings.

MOTHER TERESA *(so happy and delighted, placing her blessingful hands compassionately on Sri Chinmoy's head):* God bless you, God bless you.

SRI CHINMOY: Every day I pray to the Lord for you. Mother, every day I pray for you.

MOTHER TERESA: Every day! And pray for our whole congregation. We are now in 120 countries, and we have 584 houses around the world.

SRI CHINMOY: I am so happy, so happy.

MOTHER TERESA: Please keep praying for us every day.

SRI CHINMOY: Every day I pray, Mother, for your health and for the success of your Mission.

MOTHER TERESA: I always have a gift to give you, which is my love.

SRI CHINMOY: You have so much to give to mankind, Mother.

MOTHER TERESA: Now I want you to pray very specially for China.

SRI CHINMOY: I am praying, I am praying, Mother.

"ARE YOU PRAYING FOR ME?"

MOTHER TERESA: You must go there.

SRI CHINMOY: I promise.

MOTHER TERESA: And one day you must come with me.

SRI CHINMOY: I shall come. Mother, I wish to offer you something very special. I have been serving the United Nations for many years. Here is a very special award from me and from the Peace Meditation at the United Nations. It says, "Mother Teresa: Humanity's Flower-Heart; Divinity's Fragrance-Soul." That is you, Mother.

MOTHER TERESA *(very happily reading the award and repeating the words with Sri Chinmoy)*: "Humanity's Flower-Heart; Divinity's Fragrance-Soul." *(Thrilled, holding the award in her lap)* For me! My goodness!

SRI CHINMOY: It is for you, for you.

MOTHER TERESA: Thank you so much. God bless you. And please continue praying for me.

SRI CHINMOY: Mother, every day I pray for you, and I shall continue doing so.

MOTHER TERESA: Thank you, thank you. *(Presenting medals from Rome)* These are some miraculous medals from Rome. They will answer prayers.

SRI CHINMOY *(after accepting the medals)*: Mother, here is a letter from President Mikhail Gorbachev of Russia for you.

MOTHER TERESA: Tell him that we have houses in Russia also.

SRI CHINMOY: President Gorbachev has sent this for you. It may be read to you by one of your Sisters at your leisure. He is a close friend of mine, so he knew I might see you. Just yesterday he sent me the letter.

Mother very happily accepts the letter from Sri Chinmoy. She opens the folder and looks at the letter.

MOTHER TERESA: Our houses in Russia are very beautiful.

SRI CHINMOY: President Gorbachev is so proud of you, Mother. He is so grateful to you.

MOTHER TERESA: What is inside the letter?

SRI CHINMOY: It is an invitation for you. Only this much I know.

"ARE YOU PRAYING FOR ME?"

MOTHER TERESA *(very happily)*: God bless him. In India we have many houses. God is so good to us. We have many Sisters, Fathers, Brothers. Pray for us; we are doing God's Work, God's Work, and you are in my prayers.

SRI CHINMOY: Always, Mother, my prayers are with you. Every day I pray for your health, and I pray for the success of your Mission. You are the choicest instrument of our Lord. The Lord Himself wants you to be here on earth for many, many more years. So you have to bless us. You have to take care of your children: humanity.

MOTHER TERESA: We are in 120 countries—can you imagine! And we have 584 houses in India and all over the world. So pray that we do well God's Work. Let the world remain in peace.

SRI CHINMOY: Mother, every day you are doing God's Work.

MOTHER TERESA: Thank you. When are you coming to Calcutta?

SRI CHINMOY: Mother, I am living here, but if I come to Calcutta, I shall definitely seek your blessingful presence. Here is some of my artwork, Mother *(presenting some books containing his writings and artwork)*.

MOTHER TERESA *(pouring her grandmotherly affection)*: All beautifully done! You must come and see me in Calcutta. Fifty thousand have died and gone to Heaven in my hands, fifty thousand people. They were all picked up from the streets, and we took care of them and loved them, and they went straight up to Heaven, to God.

SRI CHINMOY: Yes, Mother, but you were the one to take them to God. Their souls are inside your heart of blessings and love. Their souls are all gratitude to you, Mother, because you have taken them directly to the Lord with your prayers and with your blessings.

MOTHER TERESA: We have Sisters of Charity, we have Brothers, we have Fathers, we have many, many lay people. We are all praying—one heart full of love. And you pray for us also.

SRI CHINMOY: I am praying, praying, and also I am praying for something very special: that you will be with us here for many, many more years. You have to be with us to bless us, to take care of us.

MOTHER TERESA: All for the Glory of God.

SRI CHINMOY: All for the Glory of God.

"ARE YOU PRAYING FOR ME?"

MOTHER TERESA: Thank you, thank you, and God bless you. Thank you, thank you. Pray for me specially.

SRI CHINMOY: I shall pray. I am praying, praying, praying, Mother.

Both Mother Teresa and Sri Chinmoy fold their hands in farewell, and Sri Chinmoy bows reverentially before leaving the room by the door he had entered. Then Sister Nirmala introduces Sri Chinmoy to several of the Sisters.

Sri Chinmoy's third interview with Mother Teresa took place on 3 June 1997 at the Missionaries of Charity House in the Bronx, New York. Prior to the interview, Sister Nirmala most kindly greets Sri Chinmoy. He presents her with a special gift to congratulate her on her recent election as Superior General of the Missionaries of Charity.

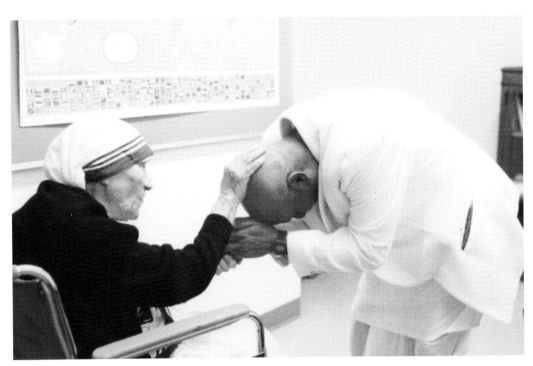

Mother Teresa, with great compassion and joy, greets Sri Chinmoy by blessingfully placing her hands on his head.

From the very start of their interview, Mother affectionately takes Sri Chinmoy's hands and lovingly requests him to pray every day for her and for her entire congregation.

Sri Chinmoy presents Mother Teresa with a specially created award on behalf of the Peace Meditation at the United Nations. The award is entitled "Mother Teresa: Humanity's Flower-Heart; Divinity's Fragrance-Soul." She is extremely happy and holds the award in her lap.

Sri Chinmoy offers Mother Teresa a letter from President Mikhail Gorbachev. The President sent the letter, which had arrived just the day before, to Sri Chinmoy, a close friend of his. He knew that Sri Chinmoy might see Mother Teresa soon. Mother receives the letter very happily and with great interest.

Sri Chinmoy presents Mother with several gifts containing his spiritual writings and artwork, including two small gift books and several bookmarks. She showers her grandmotherly affection and appreciation for the beautiful gifts.

Once again Mother affectionately takes Sri Chinmoy's hands and entreats him to pray for her. He most happily and gratefully agrees. Sri Chinmoy tells Mother that he is praying for her to be with us here and to continue blessing us for many, many more years.

— FIFTH AND FINAL MEETING —

On 17 June 1997 Sri Chinmoy and about 40 of his students arrive at the Missionaries of Charity House in the Bronx, New York City, for an appointment to see Mother Teresa. They are greeted warmly at the door by Sister Nirmala, Sister Sabita and the other Sisters, who invite them upstairs. Sri Chinmoy's students are shown into a small chapel in the front of the building.

SRI CHINMOY (*happily greeting Sister Nirmala*): O Sister, Sister!

SISTER NIRMALA (*inviting Sri Chinmoy into a small anteroom for his private meeting with Mother Teresa*): Welcome! Welcome! Please, come, come, come! How many people do you want to take for the private meeting?

SRI CHINMOY: Only one—one photographer.

Sister Nirmala leaves the room to go and get Mother. At 4:58 p.m. Sister Nirmala brings Mother Teresa into the interview room in a wheelchair.

SRI CHINMOY: Mother, Mother!

"ARE YOU PRAYING FOR ME?"

MOTHER TERESA *(vibrant and full of energy, enthusiastically greeting Sri Chinmoy):* God bless you!

SRI CHINMOY: I am so grateful to you, Mother, Mother, Mother.

MOTHER TERESA *(clasping Sri Chinmoy's folded hands and then blessing him on the head with her right hand):* Thank you.

Sri Chinmoy presents Mother Teresa with a beautiful glass shrine which shows the Saviour Christ holding a lamb and lovingly blessing a prayerful Mother Teresa. It is illuminated by a small light in the base.

As soon as she sees the Christ's picture etched in the glass, Mother Teresa is speechless. For over a minute she prays most intensely.

MOTHER TERESA *(thrilled and delighted):* Thank you! God bless you! How did you make this?

SRI CHINMOY: Your birthday is fast approaching, in August. So this gift I am offering to you on the occasion of your birthday.

MOTHER TERESA: It is beautiful with the little lamb.

SRI CHINMOY: Mother, you are the supremely chosen lamb of the Saviour.

MOTHER TERESA *(pointing to the glass lamb)*: I want everybody to be His lamb. *(She reflects for a few moments.)* Do you stay here in New York?

SRI CHINMOY: Yes, Mother. I have been here for thirty-three years.

MOTHER TERESA: Thirty-three years! *(Sincerely and lovingly)* When are you going to Calcutta? *(Speaking with the special affection and loving demand found in Bengali villages)* Come to Calcutta, come to Calcutta! Do you have a group in Calcutta?

SRI CHINMOY: Not yet, Mother.

Sri Chinmoy presents Mother Teresa with a new book that he has just written about her entitled "Mother Teresa: Humanity's Flower-Heart, Divinity's Fragrance-Soul."

MOTHER TERESA *(reading the title aloud in a firm voice)*: "Humanity's Flower-Heart, Divinity's Fragrance-Soul." My goodness!

SRI CHINMOY: This is the book I have written.

MOTHER TERESA: You wrote this?

SRI CHINMOY: I wrote this book all about you.

MOTHER TERESA: When did you write this?

SRI CHINMOY: Many things I have written recently. It also includes our meeting in Rome in 1994.

SISTER NIRMALA *(looking at the photograph in the book from Sri Chinmoy's private meeting with Mother Teresa on 3 June 1997, only two weeks earlier)*: Just the other day you came!

Sri Chinmoy and Mother Teresa look at the book together. Mother is thrilled to see Sister Nirmala's picture in the book because of her fondness for the 62-year-old Superior General, who is originally from Nepal.

SRI CHINMOY: Mother, there is more than one picture of Sister Nirmala in the book.

MOTHER TERESA *(looking at her own photograph with the Peace Torch)*: Where did I hold this torch?

SRI CHINMOY: In Rome when I came to your House for the first time.

MOTHER TERESA *(to Sister Nirmala)*: Look, look, the flame is there! Flame! Flame!

SRI CHINMOY: In Rome we sang for you.

MOTHER TERESA *(looking at the song in the book where Sri Chinmoy has set music to her words "The fruit of service is peace")*: This has become my "business card." *(Commenting on the songs composed in Bengali)* I know Bengali!

Mother Teresa continues looking through the book with great joy and delight, as Sri Chinmoy explains the different sections.

SRI CHINMOY: This is the U Thant Peace Award that I gave you in Rome.

MOTHER TERESA *(reading and looking at the book with great interest)*: Yes, yes!

SRI CHINMOY *(offering an envelope containing a donation for her Mission)*: Mother, this blessing-offering comes from the very depths of my heart.

MOTHER TERESA *(very moved, placing her hand on Sri Chinmoy's hand)*: Thank you, thank you. This is for those we pick up from the streets of Calcutta. Fifty thousand people have died in peace—no screaming, no crying, no complaining. They have gone straight to

God. They have suffered so much, but they have gone to God peacefully.

SRI CHINMOY: They have gone to Heaven, but their hearts of gratitude they have left for you here. They have left behind their hearts of gratitude.

Sri Chinmoy shows Mother Teresa a photograph in his book which shows him praying before an apparition of Mother Mary that recently appeared in the window of a bank building in Clearwater, Florida.

SRI CHINMOY: Mother, the other day I went to Florida. This is an apparition of the Mother, Mother Mary. Last week I was there. She appeared there in Florida.

MOTHER TERESA *(exclaiming over the picture)*: She appeared in Florida!

SRI CHINMOY *(while Mother Teresa looks at the song dedicated to Pope Paul VI)*: I met with him three times.

Mother Teresa looks through the section of anecdotes about her life that Sri Chinmoy had included.

SRI CHINMOY: In this anecdote, Pope Paul VI gave you his car, Mother, and then you auctioned it.

MOTHER TERESA (*after reading aloud the anecdote about the car*): What a wonderful book! This is a most beautiful book! You have my blessings.

Twice during their conversation Mother rests her hand with motherly affection on Sri Chinmoy's ailing right knee. In silence, Sri Chinmoy says, "Mother, you are curing me."

Mother Teresa continues to look through the book, commenting on the writings and the photographs. She is not wearing any reading glasses, but her eyesight is most remarkable.

SRI CHINMOY (*turning to the last page*): Mother, this is the last poem in the book. It says: "Mother, the sorrowful earth-planet has a special treasure-home, and that home is your compassion-heart."

MOTHER TERESA: Thank you.

SRI CHINMOY: This book has just come out today.

MOTHER TERESA (*noticing the dedication*): It is dated June 17th—today!

SRI CHINMOY: It was printed by my students. I have brought many copies for you and your Sisters. Would you kindly autograph my copy?

Mother Teresa lovingly signs a copy for Sri Chinmoy. She writes, "God bless you.—M. Teresa, M.C." Mother Teresa also signs a copy for Sister Nirmala. Then she signs her own copy "God bless—M. Teresa, M.C." omitting the "you."

SRI CHINMOY: I am so grateful to you, so grateful. *(Referring to the book again)* Mother, I am dedicating this to you on the occasion of your birthday.

Mother Teresa soulfully reads aloud the dedication of the book and appreciates the purple birds that Sri Chinmoy had drawn on the page.

MOTHER TERESA: God bless you!

SRI CHINMOY *(explaining to Sister Nirmala)*: I have dedicated the whole book to her. The first page, the dedication, Mother has so kindly read. The whole book is dedicated to her. My students have advance copies and they are already translating this into many languages.

SRI CHINMOY *(to Mother Teresa)*: Mother, now my students wish to sing for you in the chapel.

As they prepare to join those waiting in the Chapel, Sri Chinmoy pauses at the window.

We have collected medicine for you, Mother—ninety-eight boxes. We would like to show you the boxes.

MOTHER TERESA: Where are the boxes?

Sri Chinmoy asks Mother Teresa to come to the window to see the boxes of medicine and medical supplies that Sri Chinmoy and his students have brought. When she looks out the window and sees the huge mountain of boxes stacked on the sidewalk in front of the building, she is so happy and delighted.

MOTHER TERESA: Thank you, thank you. How much work you do for the poor and the needy—those poor in the spirit and those needy in the body!

SRI CHINMOY: It is all your sympathy, your sympathetic heart. Mother, it is all your grace. Every second you are giving your life for the poor.

MOTHER TERESA: I spend so much money on medicine. We have six mobile dispensaries in Calcutta, but we give everything free. Our poor people get modern medicine.

SRI CHINMOY: Their hearts of gratitude are inside you.

MOTHER TERESA: And those who have died are beautiful people.

Mother Teresa and Sri Chinmoy enter the Chapel, with Sri Chinmoy walking behind Mother carefully carrying the glass shrine. Sri Chinmoy's students stand up out of respect, bowing with folded hands. Mother Teresa first bows soulfully to the crucifix and then greets her guests with great joy. A number of Sisters also enter the Chapel and kneel at Mother's feet.

MOTHER TERESA *(speaking to those in the Chapel while they listen spellbound)*: In Calcutta, we have children's homes, and we give children for adoption. Altogether in Calcutta we have been able to get over 8,000 children adopted. We have done everything properly, and many families have adopted them. Now they are growing big and doing very well. Some of the children have gone to Italy and Belgium and also, naturally, India. People are very good. All those children are growing big. People are eagerly adopting them so that the child is beautifully protected.

(To Sri Chinmoy, indicating the chair by her side) Sit down, sit down!

God has been very good to us, giving us so many families to help us. If there is a young girl who is expecting a child, I bring her to our Shishu Bhavan. I want you to come one day to Shishu Bhavan, to our Children's Home. We have all kinds of babies, maybe more than 200 babies there.

Then we have a place for the dying. We pick up people from the street. We have one house where over 50,000 have died beautiful deaths. So next time you come to Calcutta, come and see me, and I will make you work very hard *(joyful laughter)*.

The people are so peaceful, so peaceful. The other day, before I came here, I picked up a man from the street. He had worms all over him. We had to pull off all these worms, and there was not a sound of complaint. He just took hold of my hands and said, "Thank you." He was beautiful, beautiful—not a word of blame or complaint. After we removed all the worms, he was full of joy.

People are very good to us. Many come and help us serve people before they die. In Titagarh we have a leprosy centre, and this is what they make *(referring to her white cotton sari)*. I pay them properly, and with that money they have a little, little house for themselves. The Government has been very good to me, giving me land, so I give a plot of land to every family. Their children are going to school, and we are preventing the children from getting leprosy.

"ARE YOU PRAYING FOR ME?"

The family spirit among them is beautiful! They work together, they love each other and help each other.

Now we are trying to open at least one house for AIDS. The new disease is spreading very fast in India. There is absolutely no medicine; they are sure to die, and it is highly infectious. It is spreading all over the world, so please pray for us, that we will be able to help them at least to die in peace with God. There is so much suffering. And their families are suffering so much. You must pray for our people so that we may be able to give the right medicine to them.

There is so much suffering, but I never hear these people curse anybody or blame anybody. They are beautiful people. The people that we take care of are Hindus, Muslims, Christians. We have houses for ladies, and for the men also. We have Kalighat, the Temple of Kali. It used to be an *ashram* [spiritual shelter] for the people who came to worship at the temple. They used to rest in this house, and the Government very nicely gave me that house.

I fill it up with only street cases. We pick up every day at least two or three. They are suffering and dying, but there is never a complaint. I have never heard them blame anybody. I have heard rich people blame, but I have never heard poor or sick people complain. I only pick up street cases in Nirmal Hriday. Then in Prem Dan we have about 300 people who are very poor people also. We feed them; we cook for 1,000 people every day. They get dal and rice, cooked very nicely, but I have never heard them complain or blame somebody.

God has been very good to me. Many people are helping me to feed the people. Then we have a mobile clinic in Calcutta which never has less than 300 patients. Taking care of them is very expensive, so any leftover medicine please kindly gather up together.

SRI CHINMOY: We shall! Mother, may they sing some *bhajans* [devotional songs]?

MOTHER TERESA: Yes, please sing!

The Sri Chinmoy Bhajan Singers devotedly perform songs about Jesus Christ composed by Sri Chinmoy in his native Bengali, accompanying themselves on harmonium, santur, flute and bells. Mother Teresa listens with tears in her eyes, smiling at each member of the group with great love. Many of those present are also moved to tears several times during the performance.

MOTHER TERESA *(deeply moved after the first two songs)*: Thank you! Beautiful! I wish I could take you one day to Calcutta. Our school people would be so happy to hear you.

(Going on to speak about the activities in her Mission) We have made a vow to give wholehearted, free service to the poorest of the

"ARE YOU PRAYING FOR ME?"

poor. We do not accept any money as payment. It is completely free service. But people are so kind and helpful, always somebody coming and feeding our people in Calcutta. We have a big place in Calcutta. Over 50,000 have died a beautiful death in Kalighat. I have never heard them grumble, I have never heard them blame somebody. There are only street cases there. Then there are separate homes for family people who are very, very poor. Then one more beautiful work we have in India: we are fighting abortion by adoption.

SRI CHINMOY *(smiling)*: Yes, they have said this about you, that you are against abortion and every day you have more and more children!

MOTHER TERESA: We have already given in adoption 8,000 children—that is how we are fighting abortion by adoption. The majority of the children have gone to Belgium and Italy and, naturally, to India. We have good support from the Government. These children are growing so big now! So I hope one day they will come and help me out *(laughter)*.

The Sri Chinmoy Bhajan Singers perform a third song, "Jishu Khristo."

MOTHER TERESA *(to Sri Chinmoy)*: You do beautiful work!

Sister Nirmala, who also speaks Bengali, is also visibly moved and delighted that Mother is enjoying the songs.

SRI CHINMOY: These are my prayerful songs to Jesus Christ. The three that they have sung are in Bengali, since I am a Bengali. They are singing in Bengali for you. Now they will sing a song that I have written about you in English.

The Sri Chinmoy Bhajan Singers perform "Mother Teresa: Humanity's Flower-Heart, Divinity's Fragrance-Soul." During the performance, two of Sri Chinmoy's students hold a banner bearing the same words along with a soulful picture of Mother Teresa. On 3 June 1997 Sri Chinmoy had presented Mother with a special award by that name.

MOTHER TERESA: Beautiful! Our people would be so delighted if you could come once and play for the people in Calcutta. All of you stay here? You don't have a group in Calcutta? How is that? (*To Sri Chinmoy*) In Kalighat people would be so happy to have them come. You do not bring them to Calcutta? (*laughter*)

SRI CHINMOY (*presenting Mother Teresa with an exquisite mandolin, since he had read in her biography that as a young girl she was an excellent mandolin player*): Mother, this is for you.

"ARE YOU PRAYING FOR ME?"

MOTHER TERESA: My goodness! For the first time in my life someone has given me a mandolin *(laughter)*.

SRI CHINMOY: You played the mandolin when you were a student. Would you like to play now? You used to play.

With great joy Mother Teresa holds up the mandolin for all to see. Then she gives the mandolin to Sister Nirmala to hold for her.

MOTHER TERESA: We are in Kalighat, near the Kali Temple. The house where we are was previously used by the people who used to come and worship. Then the Government gave us the whole house. We have picked up over 50,000 people from the streets. Nobody has died in the streets. They have a beautiful death. We help them to die with a smile. Then we have Shanti Nagar for the lepers in Titagarh.

Sri Chinmoy gives her some picks for the mandolin.

MOTHER TERESA: May I take one?

SRI CHINMOY: They are all for you.

MOTHER TERESA *(reaching for a small pile of cards)*: This is my business card.

SRI CHINMOY *(to his students)*: All of you please come.

Mother Teresa compassionately gives her "business card" with her special prayer on it to each of Sri Chinmoy's students. After taking the business card from Mother Teresa, they receive a medal of Mother Mary from Sister Nirmala. Mother Teresa explains that they are miraculous medals from Lourdes.

SRI CHINMOY *(handing Mother Teresa a framed photograph of herself)*: This picture is for Sister Nirmala. I would be so happy if you could give it to her. *(Sri Chinmoy demonstrates to Mother Teresa that when one presses this special photograph, one hears Mother's voice.)* Mother, your voice has been recorded in this picture.

Mother Teresa and Sri Chinmoy present the special gift to Sister Nirmala, and Mother comments that she sees Sister Nirmala's face inside the photograph of herself.

SRI CHINMOY: She is always inside your heart.

MOTHER TERESA *(to the group)*: Did everybody get my business card? Very good business! *(laughter)*

SRI CHINMOY: Mother, these are for all the Sisters. *(Sri Chinmoy places before Mother Teresa thirty framed photographs of herself.)*

MOTHER TERESA: They have become rich! Thank you, Sri Chinmoy, thank you. You know we have a vow with God to give wholehearted, free service to the poorest of the poor. We do not accept Government grants. We have no salary, no payment—except charity. God has been very good to us. We are now in 120 countries, and we have 584 houses. Can you imagine? God has been so good to us, and everybody is helping—Hindu, Muslim, Christian—everybody is helping. So any old saris or anything you have left over—always give to the poor.

SRI CHINMOY *(giving small, laminated cards with Mother Teresa's photograph)*: Mother, this is your new business card.

MOTHER TERESA: Oh my goodness! *(Reading her writings on the card)* "Peace begins with a smile" and "I never will understand all the good that a single smile can accomplish." My goodness! Did you all get one? These are for us? You made this?

SRI CHINMOY *(presenting fifty copies of his new book about Mother Teresa)*: These are copies of the book that I have written. They are for all the Sisters.

MOTHER TERESA: We have shared the joy of loving. We have Fathers, Brothers, Sisters. We have volunteers, and then we have co-workers. We have active lay Sisters and active lay Brothers. So many hearts are involved with the poor people. We never allow anybody to die in the street. And don't forget any old saris that you have!

SRI CHINMOY: Mother, these men and women would like to sing two songs that I have dedicated to you.

MOTHER TERESA: What is this group called?

SRI CHINMOY: These are the "Global Singers." They are from different countries.

MOTHER TERESA: Global Singers? That's why they should come to Calcutta *(laughter)*.

The Singers perform "Compassion-Mother" and "Nirmal Hriday." Mother Teresa is deeply moved and happy, specially to hear the tribute to her different houses and projects. She smiles and exclaims each time she hears the Bengali words "Nirmal Hriday," "Shishu Bhavan" and "Shanti Nagar."

MOTHER TERESA: Beautiful! Thank you! You must come to Calcutta. *(Turning to Sri Chinmoy)* You must bring them to Calcutta.
Also, we have a leprosy centre in Titagarh. They all have a plot of land and they have been given family houses. Their children are going to school. This has changed their attitude completely.

"ARE YOU PRAYING FOR ME?"

I want you to pray specially for AIDS because we have no medicine for it, and it is very highly infectious. We have to help them so that they can die in peace with God. It is terrible suffering, terrible suffering. Here in the Bronx we have a house, and in many places we have got houses to help people with AIDS. We can't get more than five or ten in a house. Thank God, they die in peace with God. It is a terrible disease. It is such terrible suffering for the family. So pray that we help them to die with a smile.

SRI CHINMOY: We shall pray for you, we shall pray for you. Now from the new book that I have written about you, Mother, some of my students will be reciting some poems.

As each of the eight students recites a poem from the book, Mother Teresa smiles and thanks each one.

MOTHER TERESA: Beautiful! Thank you very much. You must pray that we continue God's Work with great love so that we will help them to die in peace with God. I have never heard them blame anybody or curse somebody. The other day I picked up a man from the street. He was black with worms, so we had to take out the worms one by one. We helped him so much. By the time we removed all the worms, he gave me a big smile and he died.

SRI CHINMOY: It was his gratitude.

MEETINGS, CONVERSATIONS AND LETTERS

MOTHER TERESA: Yes, he gave me a big smile; then he died. I have seen many poor people die, but I have never heard them blame God. I have never heard our poor people blame anybody. It is beautiful; they help each other. We only take street cases in our home. We have another house, Prem Dan, and we have 300 people there—very, very, very poor people. Anybody that is sick and dying, we take them to our house. It is part of the Kali Temple. People used to come to that house before going to worship. Then the Government gave it to me. The Kali Mandir people are very kind to me.

SRI CHINMOY: Do you remember this incident? Once you were in a Calcutta bus. Some Calcutta women were criticising you and accusing you of converting Hindus to Christianity. Then you spoke to them in Bengali, *"Ami Bharater, Bharat amar."* ["I belong to India; India is mine."] You silenced them. They kept quiet when they heard you say, *"Ami Bharater, Bharat amar."*

MOTHER TERESA *(laughing at the recollection)*: Nobody had ever spoken to them in Bengali. They were so surprised I spoke to them in Bengali. It happened before I started this work. Now we serve only the poorest of the poor. But people are all so beautiful. I have heard many people blame somebody or something, but these poor people never blame anybody. Most of the ones we pick up are in terrible condition. But we give them tender love and care. They never scream or cry or anything. I always say, "If I were in their place, I am sure I would scream." They are beautiful.

Then we fight abortion by adoption. We have given over 8,000 children for adoption in India, not only Calcutta. But the majority, over 3,000, we have got from Calcutta. They are doing very well now. They are all over the place.

So please keep on praying for us; pray that we continue God's Work with great love. There are many young Sisters, even here in the United States. They have got a training centre to help take care of people. There are feeding centres for the hungry. Come and help us; we will feed you with very good food. And any old saris, anything, please give. I am a first class beggar! *(Sister Sabita, standing near Mother, laughs along with the audience.)*

MOTHER TERESA *(leading the Sisters in a prayer)*: We give thanks, Almighty God, for these and all Your other Benefits which, because of Your Bounty, we have received through Jesus Christ our Lord. Amen.

(Addressing the gathering) Pray for us, that we continue God's Work with a pure and humble heart so that we can help people. They are suffering, but we are assisting with tender love and care. Now that I have you in mind also, please pray that we don't spoil God's Work. And if you happen to come to India, please come to Calcutta. We have about 50 volunteers that come every day to help us with the work. The patients are in terrible condition, but I have

never heard the poor people blame somebody. So I thank God. And I will pray for you, and you pray for us.

SRI CHINMOY: Mother, I have been praying for you every day.

Nine of Sri Chinmoy's students stand in front of Mother Teresa displaying decorated signs showing some of the awards she has received over the years.

SRI CHINMOY: These are the awards you have received.

✣ POPE JOHN XXIII PEACE PRIZE, 6 January 1971, Vatican City

✣ PADMA SHRI, April 1962, New Delhi, India

✣ JAWAHARLAL NEHRU AWARD FOR INTERNATIONAL UNDERSTANDING, 15 November 1972, New Delhi, India

✣ TEMPLETON AWARD, 25 April 1973

✣ ALBERT SCHWEITZER INTERNATIONAL PRIZE, 1975

✣ NOBEL PEACE PRIZE, 1979, Oslo, Norway

✣ BHARAT RATNA, 22 March 1980, New Delhi, India

"ARE YOU PRAYING FOR ME?"

✤ HONORARY CITIZEN OF AMERICA, 1996 (only the fourth person in history to be so named)

✤ CONGRESSIONAL MEDAL OF HONOR, 1997, United States

MOTHER TERESA *(reading the names of each of the awards with great joy, especially exclaiming at the Nobel Prize):* Beautiful! What trouble you have taken! Thank you so much. I am a great friend of our Government. They have helped me a lot.

SRI CHINMOY: I understand Jyoti Basu, the Chief Minister of West Bengal, helps you immensely.

MOTHER TERESA: Jyoti Basu is my friend.

SRI CHINMOY: He is a communist who does not believe in God, but you can go to his office at any time.

MOTHER TERESA: Any time, any time! If we need immediate help, or if I need something signed, I go, and immediately he signs it. He knows where it is going. He has come a few times to see the people and the children. We have Shishu Bhavan, and we have five schools in Calcutta for street children. We bring them up to class two, and then we send them to regular schools. So there is a future for them—young boys and girls. We have all kinds of things. And we have a typing class. So they will be a little bit educated, and they can get good jobs.

So pray for us that we continue God's Work, and I will pray for you that you grow in great love for God and spread that love everywhere you go. Thank you very much. If you come to Calcutta, you must come to our place.

Mother Teresa is taken through one of the doors, while the Sisters start preparing for the six o'clock Mass in the chapel.

SRI CHINMOY *(thanking Sister Sabita for her kind assistance)*: Sister Sabita! I have a student with the same name, Savita. The other day you spoke to her, but she did not dare to announce her name. When you called, she answered the phone.

At 6:02 p.m., as they leave the building, Sri Chinmoy and his students thank the Sisters.

SISTER NIRMALA *(standing in the doorway and saying good-bye to each individual)*: It was absolutely Heavenly for Mother and for all of us! To be with Sri Chinmoy and all of you tonight was pure joy! Wonderful, just wonderful!

* * * * *

"ARE YOU PRAYING FOR ME?"

Sri Chinmoy's comments after the meeting:

In Mother Teresa I see so much of Mother Mary. Although Jesus Christ is her life-breath, I feel in her Mother Mary's compassion and forgiveness aspects. Here is one daughter of whom Mother Mary can truly be proud! Mother Mary has found quite a few sons to carry her message to the four corners of the globe, but she has not found other daughters to carry her message in the same way. No other nun or female Christian missionary has established a worldwide mission like Mother Teresa. Down the centuries, men have gone from here to there in the name of Mother Mary. But the way Mother Teresa has gone all over the world—here, there, everywhere—no other woman has done this for Mother Mary. That is why Mother Mary must have very special affection, very special love, very special blessings and very special pride for Mother Teresa. Other women saints have prayed and have been very spiritual, but their works have been limited to a particular town or city or village. Here, in her case, the whole world she has covered. Is there any place she has not gone!

In the Christ's case, there came a time when He entered into the justice-world. But in Mother Mary's case it was not like that. Who is a sinner, who is a saint? God alone knows. It does not matter, as long as She can bless everyone—that is Mother Mary.

The father aspect judges, but the mother aspect never judges. No matter how bad, how undivine her child is, the mother loves him.

The father will judge whether someone is a good fellow or a bad fellow, whether he is illiterate or a man of knowledge. But everybody has passed the mother's examination. As long as you call her mother, she is satisfied! You do not have to get a master's degree. She does not care for what her child is doing. But the father will ask, "Is he an idiot or a learned man?" The mother is not going to ask even what profession he has. As soon as you say, "Mother, I come for your blessings," she is all love and compassion.

Our meeting with Mother Teresa was like a family chat. She spoke to us without any reservations. Mother Teresa has one hundred per cent Indian vibration. She is like our beloved elderly Bengali village women, so full of love, affection, simplicity and wisdom. It was like a grandmother giving a lecture to her grandchildren. Many times she repeated herself, but the things that she was saying are her mantras. She only says what is in her heart. When she says something, she knows that everybody is not paying attention at the same time. That is why she repeats it a second time and a third time. She does not know at what point somebody's consciousness will be high enough to identify themselves with her mantra. The first time one person will respond, the second time another person will respond, and so on. She is saying, "Feed the poor, serve the needy, love everybody." This is her life's mantra, her life's message.

Many times during our meeting I felt that the room was filled with the ecstasy-flooded presence of the Saviour Christ.

4:50 pm, 17 June 1997. Sri Chinmoy meditates outside the Missionaries of Charity House in the Bronx, New York, just before his fifth meeting with Mother Teresa. The 98 boxes stacked beside him contain medical supplies which Sri Chinmoy and his students had collected to assist Mother Teresa in her work for the poor. They are arranged so that Mother can view them from her upstairs window.

Sri Chinmoy is greeted at the door by Sister Sabita, whom Mother has appointed head of the Bronx House.

Mother Teresa greets Sri Chinmoy and most lovingly and compassionately blesses him.

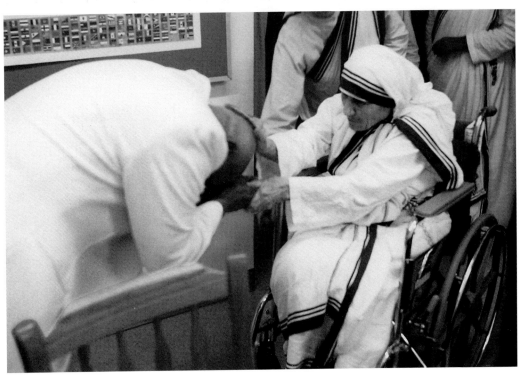

Sister Nirmala wheels Mother to the table where Sri Chinmoy unveils his gift for her: a glass shrine on which is etched a portrait of Jesus Christ cradling a lamb. In the lower right-hand corner, Mother's portrait appears. She is praying devotedly to her Lord with folded hands. Sri Chinmoy turns on a small switch in the base which causes the shrine to be illumined.

Pointing to the lamb, Mother says: "I want everybody to be His lamb." She is extremely happy. On the wall there is a picture of Pope John Paul II blessing Mother Teresa.

Sri Chinmoy presents Mother and Sister Nirmala with his new book: *Mother Teresa: Humanity's Flower-Heart, Divinity's Fragrance-Soul.* They look through it eagerly, commenting on many of the poems, photographs and anecdotes that it contains.

A picture of the Holy Father draws a smile from Mother.

A special look of love and gratitude passes between two God-servers.

Mother gathers all the books together to autograph them.

Mother most compassionately signs her blessings in the author's own copy.

Mother gazes through the window at the mountain of medical supplies in the street below and offers her prayerful gratitude.

Upon entering the chapel after Sri Chinmoy's private meeting with her, Mother Teresa soulfully bows to the Saviour. His words "I Thirst" are inscribed in every chapel of the Missionaries of Charity. In her constitution, Mother wrote: "Our aim is to quench the infinite thirst of Jesus Christ on the cross by dedicating ourselves freely to serve the poorest of the poor."

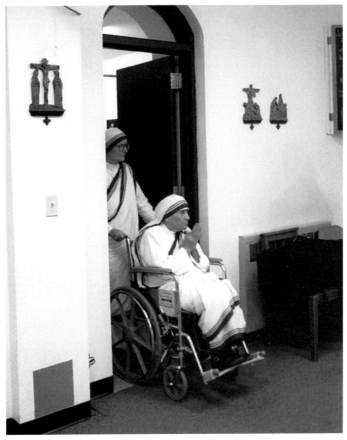

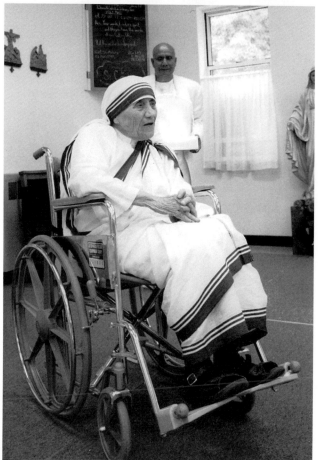

Mother Teresa warmly greets Sri Chinmoy's students, while Sister Nirmala smiles sweetly by her side. Meanwhile, the Sisters kneel at Mother's feet to receive her blessings and love. They know that in a matter of a few days she will return to Calcutta.

With utter humility, simplicity and joy Mother describes her life's philosophy and work. Sri Chinmoy's students listen with brimming tears to her words and bask in her compassionate presence.

The Sri Chinmoy Bhajan Singers perform *bhajans* that Sri Chinmoy has composed for the Christ in the Bengali language, as well as a song in English dedicated to Mother Teresa. The words to the song appear on the banner.

Mother Teresa listens to the music with soulful attention and spontaneous delight.

Sri Chinmoy hands the glass shrine to Sister Nirmala for safekeeping, and she holds it most tenderly and lovingly.

To Mother's astonishment, Sri Chinmoy presents her with a mandolin. He had come to learn that in her youth she was an excellent mandolin player. Mother is also gifted with a beautiful soprano voice and, as a young girl, she and her sister were known as the church's two nightingales.

Mother Teresa offers each person her "business card" which contains the words to her prayer: "The fruit of service is peace."

Sister Nirmala, standing by Mother's side, then distributes miraculous medals of Mother Mary from Lourdes.

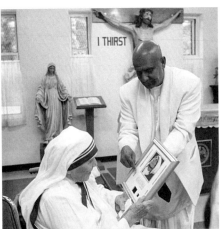

Sri Chinmoy's next gift is for Sister Nirmala. It is a framed photograph of Mother Teresa. When a certain button inside the frame is pressed, a recording of Mother's own voice plays. Sri Chinmoy lovingly requests Mother to give this gift to Sister Nirmala. He has also prepared smaller framed photographs of the Mother as gifts for each of the Sisters.

Sri Chinmoy offers Mother some small laminated cards that he has made specially for her. They carry two of her sayings together with one of her beautiful, smiling photographs. The two quotations are: "Peace begins with a smile," and "I never will understand all the good that a single smile can accomplish."

Mother deeply enjoys Sri Chinmoy's song for her entitled "Compassion-Mother." It is sung by the Sri Chinmoy Global Singers.

A small group recites poems for Mother from Sri Chinmoy's new book.

As the meeting draws to a close, Mother Teresa leads her Sisters in a special prayer of gratitude to God for His infinite Bounty.

A view of the Sisters enjoying the presentations and musical performances.

Sri Chinmoy offers his gratitude to Sister Sabita for receiving him and his students at the Bronx House.

As a final gesture, some of Sri Chinmoy's students display placards bearing the names of some of the many honours and awards which Mother Teresa has received during her lifetime. The foremost among these is the Nobel Prize for Peace awarded to her in 1979.

Happiest memories of Mother's radiant smile.

After more than one hour in Mother's compassion-affection-flooded presence, Sri Chinmoy bows in a final farewell.

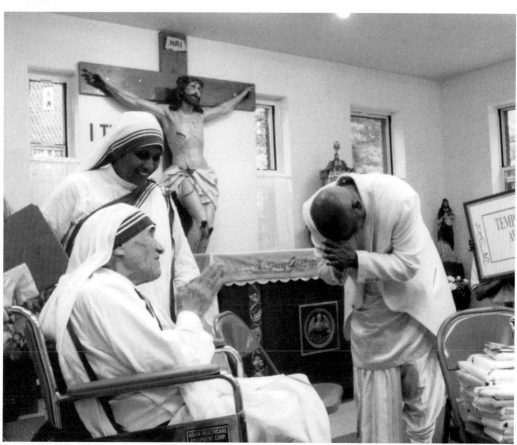

— TELEPHONE CALL FROM MOTHER TERESA
ON THE MORNING OF HER DEPARTURE FOR CALCUTTA —

27 June 1997

At Mother Teresa's request, Sister Sabita of the Missionaries of Charity in the Bronx, New York, telephoned Sri Chinmoy at 11:40 a.m. on Friday, 27 June 1997—the day of Mother's departure for Calcutta. Sri Chinmoy, who was not expecting to receive a call at that time, was utterly surprised when Sister Sabita announced her name.

SISTER SABITA: Sri Chinmoy, this is Sister Sabita. I have received your book. *(She is referring to Sri Chinmoy's book* The Son, *a full-length play about the life of the Saviour Christ.)* Thank you very much.

SRI CHINMOY: Sister, although I am a Hindu, I have the utmost devotion for the Saviour Christ.

SISTER SABITA *(very happy in her expression)*: Mother is waiting for you, Sri Chinmoy. Mother wants to speak to you. Mother is leaving for Calcutta today.

MOTHER TERESA: Sri Chinmoy, Sri Chinmoy! God bless you. God bless you.

"ARE YOU PRAYING FOR ME?"

SRI CHINMOY *(surprised and delighted to hear Mother's voice)*: Mother, how are you?

MOTHER: I am much, much, much better.

SRI CHINMOY: Mother, Mother, I want to receive blessings from you before you go. Mother, you are going today and I am so happy that before you leave you are blessing me. I am so grateful to you. Mother, did you get a chance to read my book that I wrote for your birthday?

MOTHER TERESA *(with tremendous enthusiasm)*: Yes! Again I have read your book, page by page. I have enjoyed it very much! You have taken such labour.

SRI CHINMOY: It is all my love and gratitude to you, Mother.

MOTHER TERESA: Now listen—you have to pray for me every day.

SRI CHINMOY: Mother, I do. Every day I pray for you.

MOTHER TERESA: You have to pray also for my people—poor people and dying people. You have to pray for them. Thousands of people are suffering every day and thousands are dying. I want you to pray for all of them—for dying people and for suffering people.

SRI CHINMOY: Mother, Mother, I am praying. I am praying to the Saviour Christ for these suffering people and dying people. I am sure all those who are dying are leaving behind their gratitude inside your heart. They are going to Heaven, but they are keeping their gratitude to you inside their heart.

MOTHER TERESA: Now listen! I want to open up a House in China. I want you to come with me.

SRI CHINMOY: Mother, I shall definitely accompany you to China. I am praying to the Saviour Christ to keep you for many more years here on earth so that He can work in and through you. He will definitely open up a House in China for you. Mother, you now have a House in Russia.

MOTHER TERESA *(with divine pride in her voice)*: One House! I have four Houses. I have four Houses, not one!

SRI CHINMOY: Mother, I am so happy to learn that you have four Houses in Russia.

MOTHER TERESA: Now I want to have a House in China. China needs light.

SRI CHINMOY: Mother, definitely China needs light. China needs God's Light.

MOTHER TERESA: Pray for me. Pray for my people. Pray for me. Pray for my people.

SRI CHINMOY: Mother, I am so happy that you are blessing me before you leave for Calcutta today. Mother, I need your blessings.

MOTHER TERESA: I am blessing you. I am blessing you. God bless you. God bless you.

At the conclusion of Mother Teresa's farewell call, Sri Chinmoy reflected that for the very first time she had said to him, "I am blessing you, I am blessing you." Usually she always said, "God bless you." Sri Chinmoy was profoundly moved to receive Mother's blessings.

— LETTER FROM MOTHER TERESA —
WRITTEN ON THE AFTERNOON OF HER DEPARTURE FOR CALCUTTA —

 "As long as you did it to one of these My least brethren. You did it to Me"

335 East 145th Street
Bronx, New York 10451
June 27, 1997

Dear Sri Chinmoy,

Thank you for all you are to God, for the beautiful work you have done for the glory of God and the good of souls.

I keep you in my prayer and I count on your continual support through your prayers and sacrifices that we may do God's work with great love for His greater glory.

God bless you
M Teresa mc

— LAST TELEPHONE CONVERSATION BETWEEN SRI CHINMOY AND MOTHER TERESA —

26 August 1997 – New York time
27 August – Calcutta time

From New York, Sri Chinmoy called Mother Teresa in Calcutta on the evening of 26 August, New York time. In Calcutta, it was 9:10 a.m. on the morning of 27 August. The date of Mother Teresa's physical birthday is 26 August, and 27 August is the date of her baptismal or spiritual birthday. This was her 87th birthday. The day of Sri Chinmoy's 66th birthday was also 27 August. Because she knew that Sri Chinmoy would be calling at a given time, Mother Teresa herself answered the phone when he called. Otherwise, Mother was not answering the phone herself.

MOTHER TERESA: Hello!

SRI CHINMOY: Mother, this is Sri Chinmoy calling from New York. How are you, Mother?

MOTHER TERESA *(with tremendous joy)*: Oh, Sri Chinmoy! Sri Chinmoy! Thank God! I am much, much better. I have been out of town.

SRI CHINMOY: Happy, happier, happiest birthday, Mother!

MOTHER TERESA: Ah! You know it is my birthday!

SRI CHINMOY: Mother, who does not know that it is your birthday! When the sun shines, the whole world knows that the sun is shining! I am praying to the Saviour Christ to grant you His very, very special Blessings on your birthday. You came into the world to do something really great, and you have been doing that through your sleepless service to humanity. Mother, you have to stay here on earth for many, many years to continue blessing your loving children.

MOTHER TERESA: All for the Glory of God! How are you, Sri Chinmoy? How are you?

SRI CHINMOY: I am doing very, very well, Mother.

MOTHER TERESA: Thank God! Thank God!

SRI CHINMOY: Mother, the advice which you have been giving to the Indian Government on India's 50th Independence celebrations is so inspiring and illumining.

MOTHER TERESA: Praise God!

SRI CHINMOY: Mother, have you received my letter which I sent you about fifteen days ago? As my love-offering to you on the most auspicious occasion of your birthday, I have also sent you a check.

MOTHER TERESA (*very, very happy*): Thank God! That is beautiful! Every day we feed so many people. This is a wonderful gift of love! Thank you! I will ask our Sisters if it has been received.

SRI CHINMOY: Mother, I am so blessed that my birthday falls on the same day as your birthday! You are the ocean and I am a tiny drop.

MOTHER TERESA: I am so happy that our birthdays are on the same day! God bless you, Sri Chinmoy. From the time I have come to know you, I have been praying for you every day. All of my Sisters and I shall pray for you most specially on your birthday. You must also pray for us. We must keep doing the right thing.

SRI CHINMOY: Mother, I am praying for you most devotedly each and every day and for your Missionaries of Charity all over the world. My students from many countries are also praying for you every day.

MOTHER TERESA: Wonderful! All that you are doing for the world is for the Glory of God and the good of people! Pray for me, as I pray for you and for all of your many projects for world peace. Your works of love are works of prayer, and your works of prayer are works of God.

SRI CHINMOY: Thank you, Mother! I am extremely grateful to you. I shall continue praying for you without fail.

MOTHER TERESA: God bless you, Sri Chinmoy.

— TELEPHONE CONVERSATION —

1 September 1997

On 1 September 1997 one of Sri Chinmoy's students telephoned Mother Teresa with Sri Chinmoy's humble request for her to offer a special message on the death of Princess Diana that could be read out at a Peace Concert Sri Chinmoy would be offering in memory of the Princess at the United Nations in early October.

MOTHER TERESA: How wonderful that Sri Chinmoy is holding a prayer service at the United Nations for Diana! She used to come to our Missionaries of Charity here in Calcutta. She visited Kalighat and all of our places. Pray for Diana, pray for the reposal of her soul. I am praying for Diana....

I am feeling much better. Tell Sri Chinmoy to pray for me. Please ask Sri Chinmoy to keep praying for us. Thank God that he is praying for us specially that we may open a House in China. Very wonderful! God has done many miracles for us. Now we are praying for one more miracle. God bless Sri Chinmoy!

Mother gave this blessingful message just four days before her own final departure.

All-Conquering Compassion

SONG-OFFERINGS TO MOTHER TERESA

COMPASSION-MOTHER

Words and music
by Sri Chinmoy
3 February 1994

(continued)

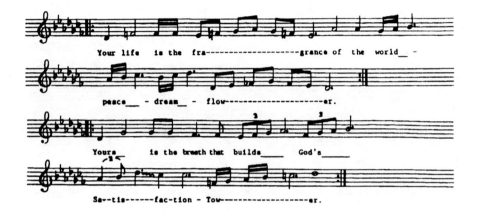

COMPASSION-MOTHER

Affection-Sister, Compassion-Mother Teresa divine,
Every day God's Smile, Joy and Pride with your soul dine.
Mother, your Calcutta's streaming tears
   And bleeding heart you are.
To you the whole world bows and bows from near and far.
Your life is the fragrance of the world-peace-dream-flower.
Yours is the breath that builds God's Satisfaction-Tower.

NIRMAL HRIDAY

**Words and music
by Sri Chinmoy
4 February 1994**

Sing once with repeats,
once without repeats,
then D.C. al fine with repeat.

NIRMAL HRIDAY

Nirmal hriday nirmal hriday
Devi Teresar karuna abhoy
Nirmal shishu bhavan
Mayer tyager jiban
Ogo shanti nagar shanti nagar
Devi mata Teresar bijoy amar

Translation:
O purity-heart, O purity-heart,
You are goddess Teresa's all-conquering compassion.
O purity-children's home,
You are Mother's sacrifice-life.
O peace-town, O peace-town,
You are goddess Mother Teresa's victory immortal.

Notes:
Nirmal Hriday: The name of Mother Teresa's Home for the Dying in Calcutta
Shishu Bhavan: The name of Mother Teresa's Children's Home in Calcutta
Shanti Nagar: The town for lepers that Mother Teresa established on 34 acres of land outside Calcutta

The Bengali language in which this song is written is Sri Chinmoy's mother tongue and Mother Teresa's adopted tongue. She spoke it fluently.

MOTHER TERESA: HUMANITY'S FLOWER-HEART, DIVINITY'S FRAGRANCE-SOUL

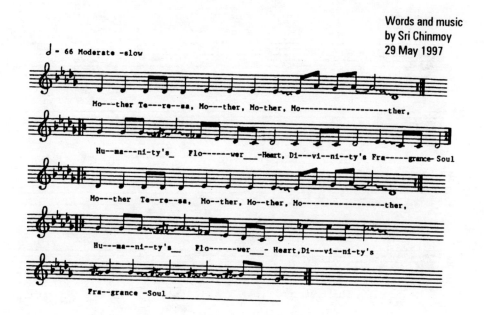

Mother Teresa, Mother, Mother, Mother:
Humanity's Flower-Heart,
Divinity's Fragrance-Soul

Note:
This is the name of the special award that Sri Chinmoy presented to Mother Teresa on 3 June 1997 on behalf of the Peace Meditation at the United Nations.

THE FRUIT OF SERVICE IS PEACE

THE FRUIT OF SERVICE IS PEACE

The fruit of silence is prayer.
The fruit of prayer is faith.
The fruit of faith is love.
The fruit of love is service.
The fruit of service is peace.

– *Mother Teresa*

Note: This is the text on Mother Teresa's "business card."

ALL WORKS OF LOVE

Words by Mother Teresa
Music by Sri Chinmoy
26 July 1995

All works of love are works of peace.

IF YOU JUDGE PEOPLE

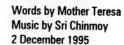

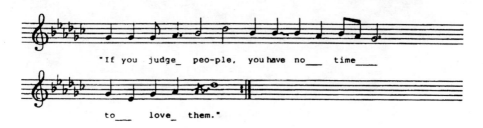

If you judge people, you have no time to love them.

I DO NOT PRAY FOR SUCCESS

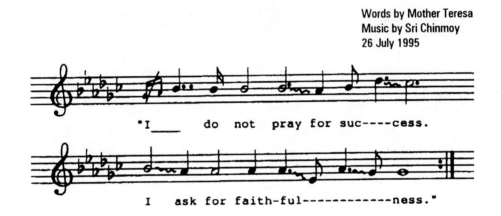

I do not pray for success.
I ask for faithfulness.

I AM A LITTLE PENCIL

I am a little pencil in the Hand of a writing God,
Who is sending a love letter to the world.

GOD HAS NOT CALLED ME

Words by Mother Teresa
Music by Sri Chinmoy
26 July 1995

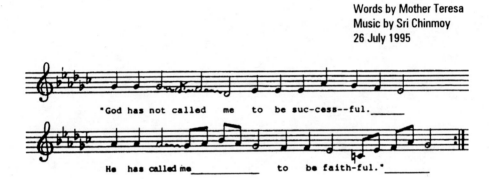

God has not called me to be successful.
He has called me to be faithful.

AMI BHARATER BHARAT AMAR

AMI BHARATER BHARAT AMAR

"Ami Bharater Bharat amar"
Amar hriday Bharat prachar
"Ami Bharater Bharat amar"
Charane sanpinu jiban amar
"Ami Bharater Bharat amar"
Bharater joy gahi charidhar

Translation:
"I belong to India; India is mine."
My heart is for the declaration of her message.
"I belong to India; India is mine."
I surrender my life at her feet.
"I belong to India; India is mine."
I sing India's victory-song
   In the four corners of the globe.

From the following incident, Sri Chinmoy got the inspiration to write the song "Ami Bharater Bharat Amar."

Silence-flooded is Mother Teresa's life, and the source of this silence is her sleepless and breathless prayer to God. But again, when necessity demands, she silences the roaring, thundering, criticising and whispering, stupid humanity. Once when she was in a Calcutta tram, she overheard a few Bengali ladies criticising her ruthlessly. They were saying that this foreign lady had come to their country only to convert everybody to Christianity. They were hurling their criticism-arrows at her in Bengali. They did not realise that Mother Teresa could speak their language fluently.

Mother Teresa's immediate response in her self-defence silenced them. She said, gently but firmly: *"Ami Bharater, Bharat amar."* (I belong to India; India is mine.) The Bengali ladies were compelled to bow their heads low.

To our great joy, Mother Teresa is fluent in five languages: English, Bengali, Hindi, Albanian and Serbo-Croatian. The philanthropist and the linguist in her enjoy their inseparable oneness.

SONGS AND MEDITATIONS
ON THE SAVIOUR CHRIST

JISHU JISHU NAM

Words and music
by Sri Chinmoy
2 May 1976

♩ = 120 Moderate

Ji - shu ji - shu nam Ja - pi a - bi - ram
Ji - shu che - ta - nai Pran___ du - be jai
Ji - shu sa - ba - kar Pi - tar dha - rar

*Jishu Jishu nam
Japi abiram
Jishu chetanai
Pran dube jai
Jishu sabakar
Pitar dharar*

Translation:
We meditate on the Christ.
We repeat His Name countless times.
Without the Christ-consciousness,
Our life is totally lost.
Christ is for all.
He is our Divinity's Son
And humanity's Father.

Note: *Jishu* is the Bengali word for Jesus.

AMI SHISHU / I AM A CHILD

Ami shishu ami shishu
Ami chira shishu
Meri kole dhara buke
Jatha chhila Jishu

Translation:
I am a child, I am a child,
An eternal child,
Like Jesus on the lap
Of Mary on earth.

JISHU TUMI DYULOKER SHISHU

Jishu Jishu Jishu Jishu
Tumi dyuloker shishu
Dhara kalyan lagi
Raye acho sada jagi

JISHU KHRISTO

Words and music
by Sri Chinmoy
22 December 1988

*Jishu Khristo Jishu Khristo
Jishu Khristo
Tumi moder baroy apan
Baroy mista*

FATHER, FORGIVE THEM

Sacred utterance of Jesus Christ
Music by Sri Chinmoy
10 December 1981

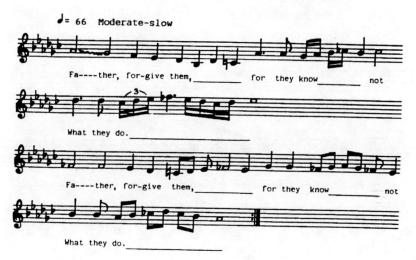

Father, forgive them,
For they know not
What they do.

Luke 23:34

I AND MY FATHER ARE ONE

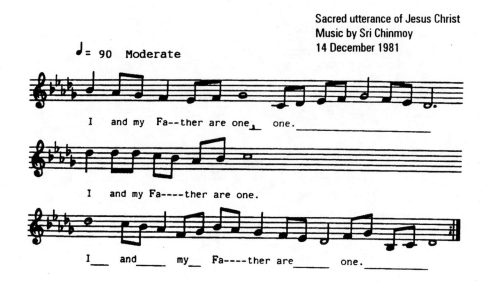

I and my Father are one.

John 10:30

NOT MY WILL, BUT THINE BE DONE

Not my will,
But Thine be done.

Luke 22:42

Meditations on the Saviour Christ

The Christ told the Truth.
The Truth existed before.
The Christ became the Truth.
Hence the Truth lives and breathes on earth.

Jesus was great.
Greater was His mercy.
Greatest was His sacrifice.

The external Christ is the mystery.
The inner Christ is the history.

Human evolution greeted the descending Christ.
Divine glorification greeted the ascending Christ.

The human Christ represented the process of Life.
The divine Christ represented the success of Truth.

In His baptism, the Christ realised the Truth for the second time.
In His crucifixion, the world realised Him for the first time.

Three fleeting years between His baptism and His crucifixion. But during this strikingly short period, His Father could and did say what He had intended to say through His Son's lips.

It is not under the branches, but at the foot of the tree that one gets full protection. Therefore human souls, wherever they may be scattered, return to their families to breathe in serenely the universal harmony and peace on Christmas.

ALL-CONQUERING COMPASSION

Jesus came. The world heard.
Jesus went. The world saw.
Jesus smiles. The world becomes.

Jesus wanted. The world gave not.
The world wanted. Jesus gave. In addition, He became.

Jesus had the chance to tell the world the matchless virtue of forgiveness.

Jesus did not have the chance to tell the world the unavoidable necessity of the sword.

Jesus' human birth was the question.
His divine Death was not only an answer, but The Answer.

ALL-CONQUERING COMPASSION

God was more than successful in sending down His Son to the earth.
Humanity suffered worse than defeat in not receiving the Son.

Jesus had. The world needed.
The world had. Jesus accepted.

Jesus did. He unveiled Himself.
The world did. It veiled itself.

God smiled through Jesus' eyes.
Humanity cried through Jesus' eyes.

ALL-CONQUERING COMPASSION

Jesus' body showed the earth how to rise.
Jesus' soul showed the Heavens how to descend.

Earth's blunders are great.
God's Compassion is greater.
Jesus knew it.
He prayed for this blessing: "Father, forgive them, for they know not what they do."

I saw the face
   Of the suffering Christ.
      I cried and cried.

I felt the heart
   Of the forgiving Christ.
      I smiled and smiled.

I clasped the soul
   Of the illumining Christ.
      I danced and danced.

IN PRAISE OF MOTHER MARY

On 13 June 1997, Sri Chinmoy prays before an apparition of Mother Mary that recently appeared in the window of a bank building in Clearwater, Florida.

OUR LADY, QUEEN OF PEACE

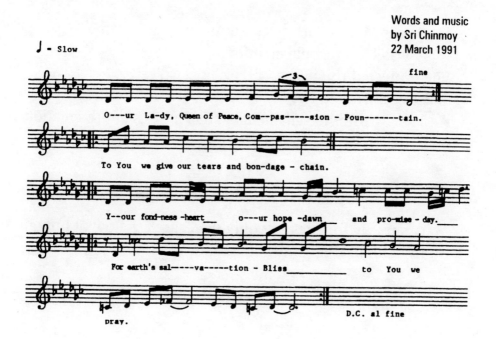

Our Lady, Queen of Peace, Compassion-Fountain,
To You we give our tears and bondage-chain.
Your Fondness-Heart, our hope-dawn and promise-day.
For earth's Salvation-Bliss to You we pray.

Meditations on Mother Mary

Jesus was Mary's earthly creation.
Mary was His spiritual creation.
She protected the plant.
The tree sheltered her.
And she within herself shelters His Father's entire creation.

Mary's purity touches not only the ceaseless flow of human impurity, but also its fount: ignorance.

Human impurity knows only how to cry out. Mary's divine purity certainly listens to its cry. But her dynamic wand must wait for the Hour of God. Furthermore, the receptivity of every individual is of paramount importance.

SCENES FROM *THE SON*

ACT 1
SCENE 2

(Mary's home. Enter an angel.)

ANGEL: Mary, Mary, I have a most special message for you from Above.

MARY: Special in what sense?

ANGEL: Special in a divine sense, in an illumining sense.

MARY: Ah, then tell me, do tell me.

ANGEL: Mary, the Lord is growing inside you.

MARY: The Lord?

NOTE: This full-length play on the life of the Christ was written by Sri Chinmoy in 1973 and has since been performed all over the world.

ANGEL: The Lord of the Universe.

MARY: I do not believe you. I simply cannot believe my ears. Do not torture me, for God's sake!

ANGEL: Am I torturing you, Mary?

MARY: Yes, you are. A torrent of fear is torturing my heart. A volcano of doubt is torturing my mind.

ANGEL: Be not afraid, for that does not become you. Be not wedded to doubt, for neither does that become you, Mary. I will tell you a secret: Infinity you embody; Eternity is your heart; Immortality is your life. Jesus, the son of God, is inside you, Mary. He shall save his people. He shall rule the length and breadth of the world forever. Do you want to know how?

MARY: How?

ANGEL: He will not rule the world with the sword-power. He will rule the world with his heart-power, with his love-power.

MARY: Heart-power and love-power: are they two different things?

ANGEL: No, they are one. Heart is love. Love is heart.

MARY: At last I am really happy. You have given me the supreme message. What can I give you in return?

ANGEL: Nothing. Just believe what I have said.

MARY: I believe you now. I accept your message most gratefully.

ANGEL: Mary, your acceptance of my message is my highest reward. Mary, you are immaculate. You are great. You are divine. Mary, before I leave, I give you another piece of good news. Your cousin Elizabeth, too, will have a child.

MARY: Wonderful, wonderful! I shall visit her shortly.

ANGEL: That is a splendid idea, indeed.

(Exit Angel.)

MARY: O Lord, You are giving me Your beloved Son. I am an ignorant woman. I know nothing. But I know that You are all Forgiveness, all Compassion and all Love.

(Mary sings:)

Ah! Simple to learn my Supreme's Message-Light.
Easy to do His glowing and fulfilling Task.
In me now sings and sports His Nectar-Day.
In His Glory's sky, my Goal and I shall bask.

ACT 1
SCENE 3

(Elizabeth's home. Enter Mary.)

ELIZABETH: Mary, Mary, I have heard. But I must not call you Mary anymore. From now on I must call you Mother, Mother of my Lord Supreme. Blessed and unparalleled are you among women. Blessed and unparalleled is your son among men.

MARY: May the divine Mother, Mother of the universe, bless me, my little heart. May Her universal Consciousness guide me, my humble life. May Her transcendental Light illumine me, my small world.

ELIZABETH: I assure you, She will. The Mother of the universe will fulfil all your desires, and more.

MARY: Thank you. Thank you. Ah, I forgot to ask you the most important thing. The angel has told me that you too are being blessed with a divine child. Is it true?

ELIZABETH: Yes, it is true. But mine is no match for yours. That does not mean that jealousy will take shelter in my heart. No, never shall I allow jealousy to darken my heart's door. My son shall be the harbinger of your son's supreme arrival. My son shall tell the world who your son is. My son shall lead the world safely to your son, the Abode Supreme. He is your son, but he will be my Lord. He will be my Supreme. He will be my All.

(Elizabeth sings:)

God is a Man,
I love His Face.
His blue-gold Love,
My Heaven-bound race.

MARY: O God, do grant me three boons. I wish to see my son always the way Elizabeth sees him. I wish to feel my son always the way Elizabeth feels him. I wish to treasure my son always the way Elizabeth treasures him.

A SONG DEDICATED TO
POPE PAUL VI

22 March 1972

COMPASSION-HEIGHT

Words and music
by Sri Chinmoy
28 May 1994

COMPASSION-HEIGHT

Father, we love your eyes of glowing light.
Father, we love your heart of compassion-height.
Your soul champions love-cry for peace on earth.
You bless our weakling hearts with confidence-birth.
In you is quenched the breathless thirst of world-hours.
In you the UN's high perfection-tree flowers.

* * * * *

Pope Paul VI offered Mother Teresa a most significant gift as a sign of his blessings when he visited Bombay in 1964. When he departed from Indian shores he presented Mother Teresa with the white Cadillac which he had been using during his visit. Mother decided to raffle the car and use the proceeds for her Mission. She received the sum of 460,000 rupees from the sale of tickets.

In 1968 the Pope wrote to her personally to invite her to Rome. In his letter, he enclosed a check for $10,000 and a return air ticket from Calcutta to Rome. Mother Teresa was deeply moved by the Holy Father's blessingful encouragement and support of her work.

On 6 January 1971 Pope Paul VI assigned her the Pope John XXIII Peace Award in Rome. The Pope's most beautiful words of praise to Mother as he presented the award—one of the first major awards she received during her lifetime—resound with wisdom and truth: "She who comes to us as a Missionary of Charity is the apostle of brotherhood and the messenger of peace."

A SONG DEDICATED TO POPE JOHN PAUL II

Sri Chinmoy's first meeting with Pope John Paul II
18 June 1980

SALVATION-DELIGHT

Words and music
by Sri Chinmoy
26 November 1988

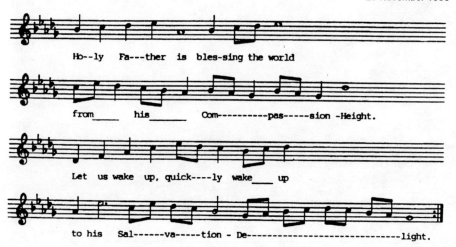

Holy Father is blessing the world
From his compassion-height.
Let us wake up, quickly wake up,
To his salvation-delight.

PART TWO

Swimming in the Sea of Tears

THE NEWS OF MOTHER TERESA'S PASSING

Around 7:30 on the evening of 5 September 1997, as Sri Chinmoy was preparing to meet with 1,700 of his students from Russia, Eastern Europe and Germany, he received the shattering news of Mother Teresa's passing. That evening, after a long period of silent meditation at the Mera Hall in Warsaw, he announced her death to his students:

Mother Teresa, dearer than the dearest for the sake of the dying people, is no more with us physically.

Just on the 26th of August I spoke to her for her blessings. She is at once my Sister of infinite affection and my Mother of infinite compassion. On our return to New York, we shall offer a memorial service for her.

Mother Teresa's very name is sanctity, simplicity and purity. Her body's death, her body's departure from the earthly scene, is a supreme loss to Mother Earth. Again, her soul's blessings for the world citizens and her inseparable oneness with the suffering humanity will always remain immortal. The goodness of her heart has covered the length and breadth of the world.

To be in her blessingful presence is to inundate oneself with humility. No matter who you are, no matter how great you are, how powerful you are, how bad or how good you are, how poor or how rich you are, just stand in front of her and all your incapacities and capacities disappear. What remains inside your heart, inside your life, is the peerless virtue: humility, reverent humility.

This year, in June, I had the golden opportunity to be in Mother's blessingful presence on two occasions. Once I had a private interview with her and once I was accompanied by some of my students. Both of these meetings took place in the Bronx, New York. Then I wanted to speak with Mother on the telephone before she left for

Calcutta. Her assistant, Sister Sabita, informed me that on the day of her departure Mother would call me and speak to me. In spite of all her pressing duties, Mother kept her promise. She called me in the morning on the same day that she was to leave New York and spoke with me for about fifteen minutes. That was not enough! Right before she left for Kennedy Airport, she dictated a letter to her assistant for me. I received the letter a few days later. That was the last letter I received from her.

Mo ther's birthday falls on the 26th of August, but she observes it on the 27th because on that day she was baptised. She gives all importance to the day she was baptised. The 27th of August also happens to be my birthday. I spoke to her for her blessings on the 26th of August, New York time. In India, it was the morning of August 27th. That was the last time we spoke. Her final words to me were, "God bless you, Sri Chinmoy."

A few days later, as you know, Mother Earth received a stupendous blow: Princess Diana left the earth-scene. Mother Teresa used to call Princess Diana "my daughter," and Princess Diana had so much affection, respect, love and fondness for Mother Teresa. Their fondness for each other was unimaginable. On 2 September, we had a memorial service for Princess Diana in New York, and for that I requested a blessingful statement from Mother Teresa. She had already issued two statements in Calcutta. At my request, she gave a third message and it was most soulful and prayerful.

After giving her message for Princess Diana, Mother added a special message for me. She said that I had to go with her to China because China needs light. So many times she asked me to go with her to China to open up a House.

There was a time, many years ago, when Mother Teresa wanted to open up Houses in Russia. When she opened up her first House, and then a second and a third, she was so delighted and excited. She felt she would be able to bring light into the Russian life. Then her sole aim became to have at least one House in China. No sincere attempt ends in vain. I am sure Mother's wish will be fulfilled under the able guidance of Sister Nirmala. Sister Nirmala is now head of the worldwide Mission of Mother Teresa. She has tremendous affection, love and concern for me. When I met her in New York, she showed me the utmost kindness.

In recent years, Mother Teresa was taken to the hospital in a serious condition quite a few times. I prayed and prayed to our Beloved Lord Supreme for her to stay on earth. At least five times, He was successful in and through humanity's prayers. But this time it was a massive heart attack. No hospital or person could be of any help to her. This time we were not given the chance to pray for her recovery.

Mother Teresa's earthly frame we shall no longer see. But her Divinity's eyes and Immortality's heart she has left behind for the world to claim as its own, very own.

As it is true that the world is full of suffering, even so, it is equally true that there came a soul to become and to remain inseparably one with the suffering humanity, and her spirit will forever remain here on earth.

That same night, Sri Chinmoy sent a telegram of condolence to Sister Nirmala in Calcutta.

```
WESTERN UNION FSI
DALLAS TX 75238
```

MISSIONARIES OF CHARITY
SISTER NIRMALA
54A ACHARYA JAGADISH CHANDRA BOSE ROAD
CALCUTTA 700016 (INDIA)

MY DEAREST SISTER NIRMALA,

MY EYES, MY HEART AND MY LIFE ARE ALL SWIMMING IN THE SEA OF TEARS. THE MOTHER GAVE EACH AND EVERY BREATH OF HER LIFE TO THE POOR AND THE HELPLESS SUFFERERS. LET US ALL OFFER OUR EVER-BLOSSOMING GRATITUDE-HEARTS TO HER. SHE CLAIMED US AS HER OWN, VERY OWN. NOW IT IS FOR US TO CLAIM HER AS OUR OWN, VERY OWN, BY LOVING AND SERVING HUMANITY SLEEPLESSLY AND BREATHLESSLY.

MY DEAREST SISTER NIRMALA,

I SHALL LOVINGLY, DEVOTEDLY AND PRAYERFULLY KEEP MY INNER AND OUTER CONNECTIONS WITH YOU AND THUS I SHALL BE ABLE TO PERPETUATE AND TREASURE MOTHER'S BLESSINGFUL WORDS, MESSAGES AND LETTERS IN MY GRATITUDE-HEART-GARDEN.

YOURS IN THE MOTHER,

   SRI CHINMOY

On 6 September 1997 Sri Chinmoy offered a Peace Concert at the Mera Hall in Warsaw, before an audience of 2,000 peace-lovers. At his request, a large picture of Mother Teresa was placed on the stage. Sri Chinmoy offered his homage to Mother Teresa and then dedicated his Peace Concert to her:

Mother, Mother Teresa, to me you were, you are and you will forever remain a Sister of infinite affection and a Mother of infinite compassion. You showered your choicest blessings, affection, love, concern and compassion upon me, upon my aspiring heart and devoted life.

With your unparalleled service-light, you have awakened and illumined millions and millions of souls that were suffering, are still suffering, and have yet to suffer. Your service-light to humanity will forever shine bright, brighter, brightest in the heart-garden of humanity.

On the strength of your sleepless and breathless service to mankind, you became, you are and you will forever remain the greatest and best treasure in the heart and life of evolving humanity.

Today's Peace Concert I am placing at your blessingful feet. You have blessed me with the beauty of infinite affection. You have blessed me with the fragrance of infinite compassion. Therefore, to you I offer my prayerful, soulful and self-giving gratitude-heart, gratitude-heart, gratitude-heart.

Sri Chinmoy then read the translation of his Bengali song "Jibaner Sheshe" and dedicated the song to Mother Teresa.

JIBANER SHESHE MARANER DESHE

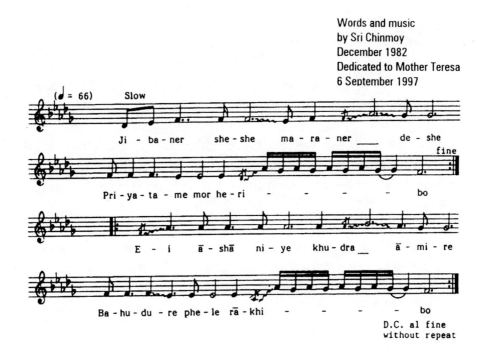

Jibaner sheshe maraner deshe
Priyatame mor heribo
Ei asha niye khudra amire
Bahu dure phele rakhibo

At the end of my journey's close,
   In death's country,
I shall see my Beloved Supreme.
Having nourished this hope,
I am casting aside my little ego-"i"
   Into a far-off land.

Calcutta's Soaring Bird

A WEEK OF PRAYERFUL OBSERVANCES

Sri Chinmoy returned to New York on the evening of Monday, 8 September. In the week that followed, he offered his prayerful tributes to Mother Teresa in words and song, as well as through a number of interviews. A day by day summary of these activities follows.

WEDNESDAY, 10 SEPTEMBER

At Sri Chinmoy's personal request, President Gorbachev and Raisa Maximovna offered a special tribute to Mother Teresa. *(p. 299)*

Sri Chinmoy was interviewed by a journalist from New York's *Newsday*. *(p. 317)*

In the evening, Sri Chinmoy answered questions from his students about Mother Teresa. *(p. 343)*

Thursday, 11 September

Sri Chinmoy wrote "My Morning-Evening-Prayer-Song" and set music to it. He dedicated the song to Sister Nirmala and sent it to her in India. He also informed her that his students would be singing it the following evening in front of churches all over the world.

He also sent a message with an arrangement of white lotuses and roses to be offered before Mother Teresa's shrine in Calcutta.

In the evening, Sri Chinmoy gave the talk "Mother Teresa-Charity-Critics Are Mental Cases!" (p. 387)

My dearest Sister Nirmala,

I have composed "My Morning-Evening-Prayer-Song" on our beloved Mother Teresa. I am most lovingly, most devotedly and most gratefully offering this song to you.

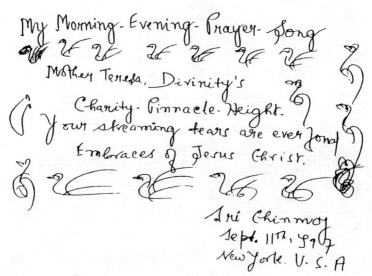

My students are going to sing this song Friday at 5 p.m. on the street in front of the Missionaries of Charity in the Bronx and in front of churches all over the world, Friday evening between 6 p.m. and 9 p.m.

Yours in the Mother,

Sri Chinmoy
Sept. 11th, 97

MY MORNING-EVENING-PRAYER-SONG

Words and music
by Sri Chinmoy
11 September 1997
Dedicated to Sister Nirmala

Mother Teresa, Divinity's
   Charity-Pinnacle-Height.
Your streaming tears are ever fond
   Embraces of Jesus Christ.

A large arrangement of white lotuses and white roses was delivered at Sri Chinmoy's request to the Sisters of Mother Teresa's Missionaries of Charity House in Calcutta to be placed before Mother's shrine on 11 September. Sri Chinmoy's attached message read:

My Sister of Infinite Affection,
My Mother of Infinite Compassion,
   My soulful promise to you is this:
I shall always remain devoted and faithful to your Missionaries and worldwide Mission.

Sri Chinmoy
New York

Ranjana Ghose, on behalf of the Sri Chinmoy Bhajan Singers, also sent a most beautiful arrangement of flowers with the message:

To our dearest Mother Teresa,

We offer you all our love, affection, admiration and adoration.

Ranjana Ghose

on behalf of the Sri Chinmoy International Bhajan Singers

Friday, 12 September

Sri Chinmoy wrote his eulogy for Mother Teresa.

At 3:00 p.m. Sri Chinmoy went to Mother Teresa's Missionaries of Charity House in the Bronx, New York, to offer flowers and a printed card with his eulogy to the Sisters.

From 6:00 to 9:00 p.m. Sri Chinmoy's students sang "My Morning-Evening-Prayer-Song" and prayed outside churches all over the world.

At 8:00 p.m. Sri Chinmoy was interviewed about Mother Teresa on "New Jersey Talking," Cablevision 12, New Jersey. *(p. 350)*

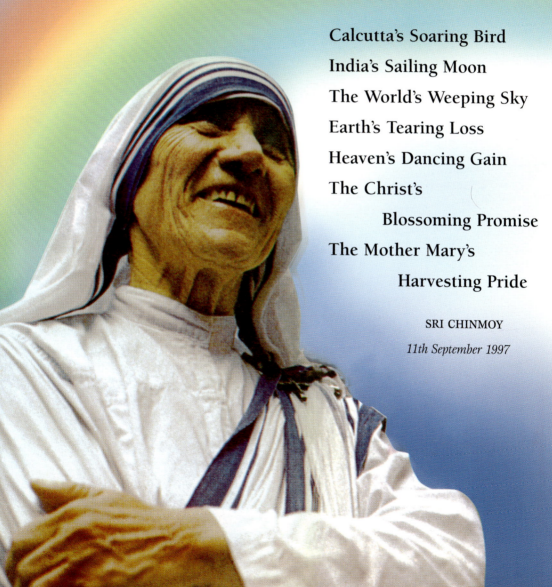

Mother Teresa:

Calcutta's Soaring Bird
India's Sailing Moon
The World's Weeping Sky
Earth's Tearing Loss
Heaven's Dancing Gain
The Christ's
    Blossoming Promise
The Mother Mary's
    Harvesting Pride

SRI CHINMOY
11th September 1997

On Friday, 12 September, Sri Chinmoy visits Mother Teresa's Missionaries of Charity House in the Bronx to place flowers before a shrine that Mother's admirers created outside the gate.

Sri Chinmoy is deeply moved by the outpouring of love and affection from the many people whose lives Mother touched in New York City.

Sri Chinmoy prays for the repose of Mother's soul.

Sri Chinmoy signs the special condolence book for mother. He writes:

Mother, Mother,
This is your Sri Chinmoy. Mother, you blessed me just the other day, August 27th, on the phone from Calcutta. Mother, I asked you how you were. You told me, "I am much better, much better, Sri Chinmoy." I told you, "Mother, your birthday was yesterday. I prayed for you most devotedly." You said: "Thank you, Sri Chinmoy. You know that I pray for you every day. Therefore, you also must pray for me every day." I said, "Mother, I do." Alas, alas, September 5th you left us for your Heavenly abode. "Mother, wherever you are, we, your devoted children, will be with you, in you and for you."

Yours in your Beloved Jesus Christ,
        Sri Chinmoy.

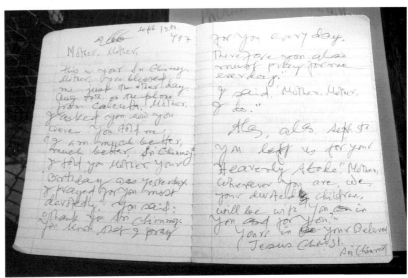

SATURDAY, 13 SEPTEMBER
(*The morning of Mother Teresa's State funeral in Calcutta*)

Sri Chinmoy set music to his eulogy of the previous day and taught it to his students.

At 7:30 p.m. Sri Chinmoy held a memorial programme for Mother Teresa at Aspiration-Ground, Jamaica, Queens, New York. (*p. 275*)

EULOGY FOR MOTHER TERESA

Words and music
by Sri Chinmoy
13 September 1997

* "tearing" as in ripping, not as in eyes tearing.

Memorial Programme for Mother Teresa
Aspiration-Ground
Jamaica, Queens, New York
13 September 1997

Sri Chinmoy offers a silent prayer and meditation before a special altar, which contains a central photograph of Mother Teresa.

The offering of votive candles to Mother Teresa's picture.

The Sri Chinmoy Bhajan Singers perform Sri Chinmoy's songs for Mother Teresa and the Christ.

Sri Chinmoy recites his eulogy and then holds up large artistic representations of each image in the eulogy.

Sri Chinmoy's students sing the eulogy while offering dramatic tableaux of each image.

Sri Chinmoy reads President Gorbachev's message for Mother Teresa.

A video is shown of Mother Teresa's life and work.

Sri Chinmoy offers his prayerful homage to Mother Teresa at a special memorial programme which he held for her at Aspiration-Ground, Queens, New York, on Saturday, 13 September. A special elevated altar, in Mother's colours of blue and white, contains garlanded pictures of the Christ, Mother Mary and Mother as well as cherished moments from Sri Chinmoy's meetings with her. A flag of India, Mother Teresa's adopted homeland, is draped over the offering table.

Sri Chinmoy invokes Mother's boundless love and compassion to bless all her world-children.

The Sri Chinmoy International Bhajan Singers offer votive candles before Mother Teresa's photograph.

As the singers sing Sri Chinmoy's special musical tributes to Mother Teresa, they are filled with sweetest memories of their meeting with Mother on 17 June, when they were blessed to sing at her feet.

Sri Chinmoy's eulogy for Mother Teresa:

Calcutta's Soaring Bird

India's Sailing Moon

The World's Weeping Sky

Earth's Tearing Loss

Heaven's Dancing Gain

The Christ's Blossoming Promise

Mother Mary's Harvesting Pride

Sri Chinmoy's eulogy for Mother Teresa is performed by a large group of singers from various countries. They are wearing white which, in Indian tradition, is the colour of mourning.

The singers create dramatic tableax to illustrate each of the seven images in the eulogy.

A dramatization of Sri Chinmoy's eulogy.

To conclude the programme, Sri Chinmoy's students file silently past the altar in memory of Mother Teresa to offer her their deepest love and respect.

The file of worshippers recalls
Sri Chinmoy's poem,
"The moment I think of Mother Teresa,
I immediately step forward
  In faith,
    In God-faith."

Sunday, 14 September

Sri Chinmoy set part of Sister Nirmala's funeral oration to music. (*p. 297*)

Sri Chinmoy's students recorded the songs he had composed for Mother Teresa.

Sri Chinmoy's eulogy was published in the *Indian Express*, India.

Monday, 15 September

At 10:00 a.m. Sri Chinmoy was interviewed by his dear friend Monsignor Thomas Hartman on Telecare Cable Television of Rockville Centre, Long Island, New York. A video clip of Sri Chinmoy's memorial service was shown and a tape of his songs for Mother Teresa opened and closed the programme. *(p. 357)*

At 1:30 p.m. Sri Chinmoy was interviewed on "Real Talk," Radio WLIB AM, New York. After answering a number of questions, Sri Chinmoy read out his eulogy for Mother Teresa. *(p. 369)*

Mother Teresa:

The Proof of God's Love

SELECTED TRIBUTES FROM WORLD LEADERS

POPE JOHN PAUL II
CASTEL GANDOLFO, ITALY
7 SEPTEMBER 1997

Dearest brothers and sisters,

In this moment of prayer, we remember our dear sister, Mother Teresa of Calcutta, who two days ago concluded her long walk on earth. I met her many times, and she lives in my memory as a tiny figure whose entire existence was the service of the poorest of the poor, but who was always full of an inexhaustible spiritual energy, the energy of the love of Christ.

Missionary of Charity: this was Mother Teresa, in name and in deed, offering such a compelling example that she attracted to herself many people who were prepared to leave everything to serve Christ's presence in the poor.

Missionary of Charity. Her mission began every day, before dawn, in front of the Eucharist. In the silence of contemplation, Mother Teresa of Calcutta heard the cry of Christ on the Cross resound: "I thirst." That cry, reverberating in the depths of her heart, drove her, on the streets of Calcutta and of the peripheries of all the world's cities, to search for Jesus in the poor, in the abandoned, in the dying.

Dearest brothers and sisters, this nun, universally known as the Mother of the poor, leaves an eloquent example for all—believers and non-believers alike. She leaves us the proof of God's Love, that transformed her life into total self-giving for her brothers. She leaves us the proof of contemplation that becomes love, and of love that becomes contemplation. Her works speak for themselves and show to today's world that high significance of life that unfortunately often seems to be lost....

While we entrust to the Lord the generous soul of this humble and faithful nun, we ask the Blessed Virgin to sustain and comfort her Sisters and those who, throughout the entire world, have known and loved her.

CARDINAL ANGELO SODANO
SECRETARY OF STATE, THE VATICAN
CALCUTTA, 13 SEPTEMBER 1997

Extracts from his funeral address:

The hour has arrived for us to say a final farewell to the late Mother Teresa. We have come here from many corners of the world to demonstrate our affection and gratitude and render a fitting homage. From the cold bier, the unforgettable, dear Mother Teresa continues to speak to us and seems to repeat the Lord's words: "It is more blessed to give than to receive."

At the close of a century which has known terrible extremes of darkness, the light of conscience has not been altogether extinguished. Holiness, goodness, kindness, love are still recognised when they appear on history's stage. The Holy Father, Pope John Paul II, has given voice to what so many people of every condition have seen in this woman of unshakeable faith: her extraordinary spiritual vision, her attentive and self-sacrificing love of God in each person she met, her absolute respect for the value of every human life and her courage in facing so many challenges. His Holiness, who knew Mother Teresa so well, wishes this funeral ceremony to be a great prayer of gratitude to God for having given her to the Church and to the world....

Dear Mother Teresa, the entire Church thanks you for your luminous example and promises to make it our heritage. Today, on behalf of Pope John Paul II, who sent me here, I offer you a final earthly farewell and, in his name, I thank you for all that you have done for the poor of the world. They are favourites of Jesus. They are also favourites of our Holy Father, His Vicar on earth. It is in his name that I place on your coffin the flower of our deepest gratitude.

Dear Mother Teresa, rest in peace.

Cardinal Basil Hume
Head of the Roman Catholic Church in England and Wales

Mother Teresa is a unique example of genuine holiness for our generation. Ordinary people around the world have been inspired by her unshakeable trust in God, her absolute commitment to the poor, and the strength of her love and humanity.

The utter sincerity with which she lived out her faith gave her an energy and a radiance which are unforgettable. Her vision will live on in all those touched by her example.

SISTER NIRMALA
CALCUTTA
13 SEPTEMBER 1997

From her funeral oration:

God loved the world so much that He sent to us Jesus Christ, and Jesus Christ loved us so much that He sent to us Mother Teresa.

We should pledge ourselves to continue what God has begun through her so beautifully. We pray that we may be faithful and truthful to the spirit that God has given to our Mother.

GOD LOVED THE WORLD

God loved the world so much
That He sent to us Jesus Christ,
And Jesus Christ loved us so much
That He sent to us Mother Teresa.

K. R. NARAYANAN
President of India

Such a one as her but rarely walks upon the earth. Though she was a world citizen, she was particularly Indian in the true spirit of our culture, and her passing away is an immense loss to the millions of our people.

МЕЖДУНАРОДНЫЙ ФОНД СОЦИАЛЬНО-ЭКОНОМИЧЕСКИХ И ПОЛИТОЛОГИЧЕСКИХ ИССЛЕДОВАНИЙ (ГОРБАЧЕВ-ФОНД)	THE INTERNATIONAL FOUNDATION FOR SOCIO-ECONOMIC AND POLITICAL STUDIES (THE GORBACHEV FOUNDATION)
125468 г. Москва, Ленинградский проспект, 49 Контактный телефон: 943-99-90 Факс: 943-95-94	49, Leningradsky Prospekt Moscow 125468 Phones 943 9990 Fax 943 9594

The Missionaries of Charity
Calcutta, India
Fax: 91-33-403788

The demise of Mother Teresa is an irreparable loss.

Her profound devotion to the Christian ideals, her love of Man, clemency, compassion, and her untiring activity in the service of humanity is an example of genuine humanism and true and active peace-making effort that Mother Teresa has set for all of us.

I am confident that the memory of Mother Teresa will always inspire all those who cherish people's good and peace.

Mikhail Gorbachev
Raisa Gorbacheva

NELSON MANDELA
PRESIDENT OF SOUTH AFRICA

I, and millions of other South Africans, were deeply saddened when we heard of the news of Mother Teresa's passing away.

Millions of our people share with the people of India and the world the sorrow and mourning of the demise of this great human being and servant of God. Mother Teresa's work amongst the downtrodden, destitute and sick will live in our memories for many years to come.

She will always be remembered for her great works of charity benefiting not only the poorest of the poor in Calcutta but also calling the world's attention to universal issues such as homelessness and poverty alleviation.

The 'Missionaries of Charity' will no doubt find strength from the groundwork laid by Mother Teresa and continue to emulate and cherish her legacy into the next millennium.

Mother Teresa's passing has also touched me in a personal way as it has been a humbling experience to have shared the similar honours of a Nobel Peace Laureate and India's Bharat Ratna with such a unique person.

TONY BLAIR
PRIME MINISTER OF THE UNITED KINGDOM

In a week already filled with tragedy, the world will be saddened that one of its most compassionate servants has died. Mother Teresa devoted her life to the poor, and her spirit will live on as an inspiration to all of us.

HELMUT KOHL
Chancellor of Germany

Mother Teresa was a model for goodness and humanity for millions of people around the world—for Christians and non-Christians alike. She helped the poorest of the poor, gave them a sense of dignity and the courage to go on living again. She gave her love and devotion to children in particular.

Mother Teresa's visits to Germany were unforgettable events. I myself am grateful for my encounters with her. She urgently directed our attention to the worst kind of poverty—the misery of people who know no love. She taught us to overcome indifference with compassion.

Mother Teresa will never be forgotten and will continue to be a model even after her death. Her memory is bound to the hope for a better, more humane world.

H. H. BIRENDRA BIR BIKRAM SHAH DEV
KING OF NEPAL

The world has lost someone who spent her whole life for the welfare and well-being of mankind. We are deeply grieved by this tremendous loss. We sincerely hope she will now rest in peace forever.

Coretta Scott King
Widow of Dr. Martin Luther King, Jr.

Our world has lost the most celebrated saint of our times. This courageous woman gave hope to millions, and showed us the power of caring and human kindness.

SAM BROWNBACK
United States Senator (Kansas)
Co-sponsor of the Motion to Give Mother Teresa the Congressional Medal of Honor (1997)

Last week, we lost a saint when Mother Teresa passed away at age 87. We are poorer, but Heaven is richer.

She died owning very few things here. She owned about two pairs of sandals, three robes, rosary beads. That was here. But in Heaven, she has a mountain of gold.

She had touched so many different lives on this Earth. It is an incredible definition of a successful life: a loving, caring, compassionate, selfless child of God, caring for, in many cases, the most downtrodden of God's children. Would that I could live my life as well.

"All for Jesus." We can all have different faiths and views of the world, but that was a driving focus for her, serving her Lord. How she did it each day is a testimony to each of us of how we should live.

We lost a saint, but the tragedy isn't that she died; the tragedy would have been had she never lived. She lived fully and gave us so much in raising our consciousness, lowering our line of sight, and redefining compassion for an entire planet. For that, I thank her and I am thankful for her life.

A Common Love of Humanity

PEACE CONCERT DEDICATED TO MOTHER TERESA
AT THE UNITED NATIONS

On 23 September 1997 a Peace Concert dedicated to Mother Teresa was offered in the Dag Hammarskjöld Auditorium of United Nations Headquarters in New York. The event was hosted by H.E. Ambassador Anwarul Karim Chowdhury, Permanent Representative of Bangladesh to the United Nations. A transcript of the programme follows.

MASTER OF CEREMONIES: Welcome to this tribute to Mother Teresa. We thank H.E. Ambassador Anwarul Karim Chowdhury, Permanent Representative of Bangladesh to the United Nations, for giving us this opportunity to share our appreciation of this humble and powerful woman. Ambassador Chowdhury, who is Ambassador of Bangladesh, Sri Chinmoy, who was born in Bangladesh, and Mother Teresa, who spoke fluent Bengali and who started her Missionaries of Charity in that part of the world, are bound together in a common love of humanity and peace.

Ambassador Chowdhury has long been an advocate for a better world through his service as Director of UNICEF's Executive Board and his participation in a wide range of multilateral conferences. He now serves his country as Ambassador and Chairman of the very important Fifth Committee of the General Assembly. We invite Ambassador Chowdhury to share with us his thoughts to begin the programme.

H.E. AMBASSADOR ANWARUL KARIM CHOWDHURY, PERMANENT REPRESENTATIVE OF BANGLADESH TO THE UNITED NATIONS: Good afternoon, distinguished ladies and gentlemen, and my respects to Sri Chinmoy. I met Mother Teresa only once, and that, too, very briefly. So I feel very inadequate to say anything about her. But it has been very rewarding for me, in my moments of difficulties, to be uplifted by her spirits, by her idealism, by her support for the downtrodden. Through her service to humanity, to the vulnerable, Mother Teresa has shown what commitment and dedication can accomplish. When we think of her, we think of purity and selflessness. Concern for the have-nots: that is Mother Teresa. Saintliness: that is Mother Teresa.

She is a reminder to us that goodness is still acclaimed in this world and that we are not yet totally given to stark materialism. Mother Teresa is a constant reminder to each of us to make our best effort every day to become a better human being. I thank you all for joining us for this remarkable Peace Concert by Sri Chinmoy, who in his life has tried to emulate Mother Teresa.

SRI CHINMOY (*After bowing to the different photos of Mother Teresa that adorn the stage*): Here is the picture of the Spiritual Summit Conference, sponsored by the Temple of Understanding, held at United Nations Headquarters in 1975, and here is Mother Teresa (*pointing to her picture*). In 1975 she came and blessed this auditorium. She was seated right here (*indicating a place on the stage*). I was extremely fortunate to have the opportunity to prayerfully offer her a rose. There were about 20 religious leaders, and after a brief meditation, I offered each of them a rose.

Mother Teresa's successor, Sister Nirmala, offered a most prayerful, soulful and fruitful prayer-message at Mother Teresa's funeral: "God loved the world so much that He sent to us Jesus Christ, and Jesus Christ loved us so much that He sent to us Mother Teresa." This momentous utterance I have prayerfully set to music. (*Sri Chinmoy sings, accompanying himself on the harmonium.*)

Sri Chinmoy then reads some excerpts from his book about Mother Teresa.

SRI CHINMOY: I spoke to her on the phone from New York nine days before she left the world, on my birthday, the 27th of August. *(He reads the conversation, in which she offered him her birthday blessings.)*

The Peace Meditation choir sings three songs by Sri Chinmoy dedicated to Mother Teresa, including one song written to her words. Members of the choir then recite aphorisms about Mother Teresa from Sri Chinmoy's book.

Members of the audience are invited to offer their personal tributes or reflections on Mother Teresa.

MS. SORAYA EMAMI: I have been doing charity work since I was 15 years old. I always wanted to go and work closely with Mother Teresa, but because I was born a Muslim I was afraid that would create a problem.

Last year I received a call from Mother Teresa at seven o'clock in the morning, California time, and she told me, "My child, you are more than welcome to come and work with me." When I went to Calcutta and spent three months working with her and with the beautiful Sisters, I experienced the joy of fulfilment and working wholeheartedly, which I had never experienced before.

The first thing I told her was, "Mother, I want to make sure I am accepted completely."

And she told me, "Anybody who wants to work with me, if you believe in God and have faith, that is all I need from you. I would rather that a good Muslim or a good Jew work with me than a Christian with no faith."

I never felt more welcome in all my years in this kind of work as during the time I worked with Mother. I will never forget the five o'clock in the morning early meditation and prayer with her all those times. I carry with me the medallion she put over my head and the blessings she offered me the day I was leaving Calcutta last November. That is going to be the most valuable thing I leave for my children. Thank you, Mother, for making me the person I am today. Thank you.

Sri Chinmoy offers a gift of prasad, with Mother Teresa's picture, to all present.

Before the programme, Sri Chinmoy offers Ambassador Chowdhury a copy of *Mother Teresa: Humanity's Flower-Heart, Divinity's Fragrance-Soul.*

Ambassador Chowdhury reflects on the life and work of Mother Teresa during his opening remarks.

On the stage of the Dag Hammarskjöld Auditorium, where he had first met Mother Teresa in 1975, Sri Chinmoy mourns the supreme loss of this beloved saint.

Sri Chinmoy points to a photograph of the programme held at the United Nations in 1975, indicating where Mother Teresa was seated during his opening meditation.

Sri Chinmoy accompanies himself on the harmonium while singing music set to an immortal utterance of Sister Nirmala, Mother Teresa's successor.

Members of the Peace Meditation choir sing three of Sri Chinmoy's songs that they were fortunate to have performed for Mother Teresa at the Missionaries of Charity House in the Bronx in June 1997.

Ms. Soraya Emami recounts the inspiring and illumining experiences she had while working with Mother Teresa in Calcutta.

Ambassador Chowdhury and his wife, Mariam, introduce Sri Chinmoy to Mrs. Khaleda Shehabudin, wife of His Excellency Mr. K.M. Shehabudin, Ambassador of Bangladesh to the United States.

My Mother of Compassion
and My Sister of Affection

LOVING REFLECTIONS ABOUT MOTHER TERESA

Following Mother Teresa's passing, Sri Chinmoy was invited by a number of media representatives to speak about his experiences with her. Excerpts from these interviews follow, along with another interview which took place at the United Nations in 1995, and Sri Chinmoy's answers to questions about Mother Teresa asked by his students on 10 September 1997.

On 14 July 1995 Mr. John Cairns and Ms. Nix Picasso, the two researchers who had collaborated with Mother Teresa on her book, A Simple Path, *interviewed Sri Chinmoy after one of his lunchtime meditation meetings at the United Nations. Sri Chinmoy offered the following reflections on Mother Teresa:*

I am very, very, very fortunate that I was able to meet with Mother Teresa last year. From my personal feeling I can say that she is both the Mother of compassion and the Sister of affection. When I look at her heart, I see that it is all compassion. When I look at her eyes, I see that they are all affection. She herself is the embodiment of both affection and compassion; these divine qualities inundate her inner being. I have the highest admiration and deepest, deepest love for her. If we had more Mother Teresas on earth, this world of ours would definitely be a world of compassion and a world of oneness.

It is because of her compassion that she accepts donations from people. For her, the one who has money is a brother, and the one who needs money is also a brother. Between the two brothers she is trying to establish the message of oneness. She sees that someone is in need and that someone else has more than he needs. So she begs and pleads with the person who has more than he needs: "Please give to me, so that I can give to our common brother, who desperately needs something." She is begging both sides. She is begging those who are not in need to give, and also she is begging those who are in need to take. Some people are ready to die in the street rather than take help from others. They have lost their wisdom or ordinary intelligence. So she has to beg them, "Please allow me to treat you. Please allow me to serve you."

To me, Mother Teresa is a living saint.

MY MOTHER OF COMPASSION, MY SISTER OF AFFECTION

During the course of a newspaper interview on 3 April 1997, Sri Chinmoy was asked which world figures he admires most. He named President Gorbachev, Mother Teresa and Pope John Paul II. In explaining his choice of Mother Teresa, he said:

In Mother Teresa I find two aspects: the mother and the sister. One moment she is the Mother of compassion; the next moment she is the Sister of affection. When I see her and talk to her, she blesses me as a mother blesses her child, and again she shows me the utmost sisterly affection.

Newsday
Long Island, New York
10 September 1997

Journalist: Ms. Merle English

NEWSDAY: I want to do a diary in the paper starting this Sunday about Mother Teresa.

SRI CHINMOY: I am still mourning my supreme loss. I have such affection, admiration and adoration for Mother Teresa, and I have received from her boundless affection and compassion. This is not the time for me to speak about myself; this is the time only to offer my deepest gratitude to her because she was so kind and compassionate to me.

She was born on the 26th of August, and she was baptised on the following day, the 27th, which is also my birthday. I spoke with her on the telephone for 15 minutes on the 26th. In India this was actually the 27th because they are one day ahead. She knew that I was going to call, so she answered the phone herself. I asked her, "Mother, how do you feel?" She said, "I am fine. I am much better." She was blessing me on the phone for my birthday, and asking me about my activities. Then she passed away on the 5th of September.

NEWSDAY: Where did you first meet her?

SRI CHINMOY: At the United Nations. On 24 October 1975 the Temple of Understanding invited religious leaders to an interfaith meeting, a spiritual summit conference, held in the Dag Hammarskjöld Auditorium of the United Nations. I offered the opening meditation and then gave roses to all the participants, including Mother Teresa. Secretary-General Kurt Waldheim was also there.

NEWSDAY: After that first meeting with Mother Teresa, did you establish some kind of connection with her?

SRI CHINMOY: It took quite a few years to build up a connection. In 1989 a student of mine spoke with her on the telephone. At that time I was completing my 25th year of service in the West. So Mother Teresa gave this message, "God bless your efforts." Since then, we have been in regular contact. In 1994 I had the great good fortune to meet with her again in Rome.

NEWSDAY: On what occasion?

SRI CHINMOY: She had kindly agreed to hold our Peace Torch. As you know, our Peace Run relay goes all over the world. Every two years the runners in our Peace Run carry the Torch through more than 70 countries.

During this meeting with Mother in 1994, I had a 15-minute private interview with her. Then she met with the forty students of mine who were accompanying me. We sang songs for her.

This experience with Mother Teresa will always remain written on the tablet of my aspiration-heart. The very first thing she did showed her real humility. I was waiting for her in a very small room—smaller than the smallest. The room was very simple, with a small table and two chairs, and it had a very sacred vibration. According to Indian tradition, out of respect I left my sandals outside the door and went inside barefoot. When she saw me with only my socks, she said, "What are you doing? It is cold in here. Either you wear your shoes, or I am going to take off my sandals also and put them outside." What was more unbelievable, she was about to pick up my sandals and bring them inside to me. So I had to walk very fast, taking long strides, towards my sandals. I grabbed them and immediately put them on so that she would not have to carry them. Then she said, "Now it is all right."

I sat in front of her bowing my head, and we did not speak for two or three minutes. We were sitting face to face. Then she took my left hand and started massaging and caressing it. After that she started caressing my right hand. When the conversation started, the first thing she told me was how she has saved about two dozen women. She told me that she had gone to a jail in Calcutta to see some women of ill fame. They had been engaging in illegal activities, and the police had arrested them. They were all crying, saying, "Mother, Mother, we did not want to lead this kind of undivine life, but we were forced to do so because of poverty."

So Mother said to them, "I am taking you back. I will give you very good training." Then Mother told the jail authorities that she would take responsibility for these women.

MY MOTHER OF COMPASSION, MY SISTER OF AFFECTION

NEWSDAY: They let the women go out with her?

SRI CHINMOY: They said, "Mother, if you take responsibility for them, we will let them go." These women all became nuns, Sisters in her Missionaries of Charity. She said to me, "This is what love can do. The world needs only love, love, love." She herself went to the jail and freed those two dozen women. Afterwards, she gave them lots of affection, and they all joined her Order. She has done this many times. When she would hear that some women did not want to lead that kind of undivine life, she would go to the jail and bring them back and transform them. She was telling me that love can transform everybody's nature, which is so true. This was her inmost conviction. This is what she started with, and to the end of her life she kept this conviction.

But in one of her writings she admitted that even love cannot change some human beings. One sad experience occurred in her life. Even with her self-giving love, she could not change the nature of one particular individual who was preventing her from entering Albania to see her dearest mother. She said, "I thought that love can do everything, but love did not succeed." Her soul's conviction that love can do everything still remained, but every rule admits of exception. So here, in this one case, in spite of trying her utmost, she was very disappointed and disheartened. She could not see her mother before her mother passed away.

NEWSDAY: After you saw Mother Teresa in Rome, you next met with her here?

SRI CHINMOY: Last year I met with her in the Bronx, and in June of this year I met with her two more times in the Bronx. On June 3rd I had a private meeting with her, and then two weeks later on June 17th, I met with her again. I was accompanied by forty of my students. They sang devotional songs for her in Bengali. She understood all the songs because she speaks Bengali. Then she invited them to come to India to sing at her Mission in Calcutta.

NEWSDAY: Did you speak to each other in Bengali?

SRI CHINMOY: We spoke in English. I would have spoken in Bengali, but she preferred English. After that meeting, I wanted to speak to her again before she left for Calcutta. One of the Sisters in charge of the Bronx House, Sister Sabita, said she would try to make the arrangements for Mother to call me. Before this meeting I had spoken to Mother Teresa several times on the phone.

On the day of her departure from New York, I got a phone call from her. She phoned me from the Bronx around 11:30 in the morning and spoke to me for about ten minutes or so. But, that was not the end. Later that same day she wrote a most compassionate letter to me. Can you imagine? Around three or four o'clock, one of the Sisters from the Mission phoned us to get our proper address, saying, "Mother has written a letter to you prior to her departure." That was her last letter, her last written blessing to me. The very last time I spoke to her was on the 26th of August, when I called to wish her a happy birthday, and she gave me birthday blessings as well. She blessed me profusely. This is what she always did.

Three or four days later, when Princess Diana passed away, I wanted to have a special statement from Mother Teresa for a book

I was writing about Princess Diana's spiritual dimension. I asked one of my students to phone her. She had already issued two statements, one for the royal family and one for the public. But she immediately gave another one at my request. That was my last contact with her. I did not speak to her directly, but I asked her for a comment and she gave one. At that time she mentioned again that she wanted me to go with her to China because China needs light. So many times she told me that I must come with her to China. She wanted us to go together to offer light. In that last contact, when she gave us a message about Princess Diana, she also said, "Tell him that we have to go to China." I will never forget this.

NEWSDAY: You were in Poland when Mother Teresa died?

SRI CHINMOY: Yes. I was watching the news about Princess Diana on television. All of a sudden, they announced that they had another piece of sad news: Mother Teresa had died. I was so shocked, because she had spoken to me only a few days earlier, telling me, "I am much better, I am much better." These were her words. O God, I was watching television with my head in my hands; I was stunned.

NEWSDAY: What do you think about the fact that these two great figures died within days of one another? One was young and one old, but they seem to have had similar hearts because Diana was trying to do some good works, and Mother Teresa always did good works.

SRI CHINMOY: Two great losses to the world, that much I can say! One Senator just yesterday said something very, very nice about Mother Teresa. He said, "We have become poorer, but Heaven has become richer."

NEWSDAY: But do you think there is any kind of message for the world in the fact that these two women died so close to one another?

SRI CHINMOY: The message is that we have to think more about the world than about ourselves. These two women have given us one message: we have to think of the rest of the world instead of just thinking about ourselves. Both of them considered the suffering, bleeding humanity as their very own. They both wanted to be of service to the poor and the suffering.

One was 36 years old, the other 87; but they died within days of one another. What can we learn from their passing? We have no idea when our time will come. So if we want to do something good for humanity, we must not waste time, but do it now. Every moment we are on earth, we can do good things for the world. Mother Teresa got an inner call, and from Albania she went all the way to India. In Calcutta she found her true home. She was living proof that the world is one home.

NEWSDAY: Did she ever talk to you about why she felt drawn to Calcutta more than to any place else in India?

SRI CHINMOY: Her Saviour Jesus Christ inspired her from within to go to Calcutta and serve Him there. She is the ocean of compassion and I am only a tiny drop, but let me give you an example of what I am saying by telling you something about my own life. I was born in India, and I spent many years praying and meditating there. I could have stayed in India, but my Inner Pilot—you say 'God', but I use the term 'Inner Pilot'—wanted me to come to America to be of service to Him here.

Similarly, she could have remained a nun in Albania, but she was prompted from deep within by Somebody to come to India. In her case, Somebody means the Saviour Jesus Christ. In my case I use the term 'Inner Pilot'. He commanded me to come to America the Beautiful to be of service to humanity. The entire world is His House. Each country is like a room. For several years I happened to live in one particular room. Then He said, "Now you must go and live in another room." So I came to this other room, but it is in the same mansion.

NEWSDAY: That is sweet—the idea that service can be offered wherever you're called, because it is all one world.

SRI CHINMOY: It is one world. If my Inner Pilot says, "You come and serve Me here," how can I say no? If I have love for my Inner Pilot—which I do—if I want to give my life entirely to please Him in His own Way, how can I have a different idea?

NEWSDAY: What memory of Mother Teresa stands out most in your mind?

SRI CHINMOY: What stood out for me from the first time I met with her privately was her compassion, affection and concern. First she wanted to bring me my sandals. Then, as soon as I sat down, she started caressing my left hand and right hand. The very first thing she shared with me was the story about the women she had saved. Her message is love and compassion. Her life-boat plied constantly between two shores, two destinations: love and compassion.

It is very easy to criticise human beings; everybody can do that. But let us see how many people can go out and work with lepers and people with AIDS. We can talk in a general way about helping the world, but if we have to face one dying person, we will not go. We do not even want to go near a hospital unless our dearest ones, the members of our immediate family, are very sick. Otherwise, even when our friends are in the hospital, we just send flowers. In Mother Teresa's case, the whole world became part of her immediate family. But Mother Teresa took people from the street, from the very gutter! Was that not her infinite love and compassion?

She is at once humanity's flower-heart and Divinity's fragrance-soul. From my personal experience I can say that this moment she was like my sister and the next moment she was like my mother. When I bowed to her, she would put both her hands on my head, like a mother blessing her son. She had every right to place her palm on my head and bless me because at that time she was playing the role of the mother. Then, the next moment, she would play the role of the sister and demand that I come to China with her to help her, or she would look at me with utmost affection. At that time she was like an older sister looking with such love and appreciation at her little brother.

NEWSDAY: She looks like a person who was very jovial.

SRI CHINMOY: Absolutely! Her divine humour was always aimed not at hurting people but at alleviating their suffering. When somebody is suffering, you can cut a joke to hurt him. Again, you can cut a joke only to relieve him of his pain. When a dear one is in the hospital, first the relatives pray and meditate for God to cure him. Then they speak to the sick person about light things, absolutely unimportant, mundane things so that they can relieve his tension. Otherwise, if they start talking about deeper philosophy, the patient's illness may only get worse!

NEWSDAY: Exactly! It will make that person feel a little bit easier. Mother Teresa must have been fond of you.

SRI CHINMOY: She was very fond of me! We have so many pictures of her pouring her affection into me. From each of our meetings we have many pictures showing how she was blessing me, showering me with her affection and appreciating my activities. Always she told me that she was praying for me every day, and she told me to also pray for her. Even on my birthday she said, "I am praying for you, and my Sisters will pray for you. You also must pray for me." Every time she spoke to me she told me to pray for her.

NEWSDAY: That is what Jesus said, too.

SRI CHINMOY: It is an emotional demand. As I said, we were like mother and son, brother and sister. So she would tell me: "You should do this, you must do this. You must come with me to China."

NEWSDAY: Was she aware of the difficulties for you to go there?

SRI CHINMOY: No, I did not tell her that. I only said, "Mother, when the time comes I shall definitely accompany you."

NEWSDAY: You met her successor, too?

SRI CHINMOY: Her successor, Sister Nirmala, is so nice to me, so kind and affectionate. When I went to see Mother Teresa in the Bronx, she came up to me and introduced herself: "I am Sister Nirmala." I had known about her, so I had brought a gift for her. She was with Mother Teresa when I gave Mother this book that I had written about her *(showing book)*. So I shall keep a connection with Sister Nirmala. I have already sent a message to her.

NEWSDAY: You gave this book to Mother Teresa?

SRI CHINMOY: It was my birthday present to her. I dedicated the book to her and gave it to her personally when I saw her in June. Then she gave her blessings for the book. On the first page she wrote, "God bless you," and put her signature there. I took that page and gave it to the printer, and it was inserted into a later edition of the book. For about fifteen minutes Mother Teresa browsed through the book in front of me. A few days later when I spoke to her, she said she had liked it very much.

NEWSDAY: You gave her this book not knowing that in a short while she would not even be around anymore!

SRI CHINMOY: If we do not pray and meditate, then we have to do everything ourselves. But if we pray and meditate, then God does everything for us. I knew nothing, but God knew what was going to happen. Why did I write the book and offer it to her as a birthday present in June? Her birthday is in August, so I should have given her the book in August. But something within me was telling me, "The sooner the better!"

When I called her on my birthday, I got her last blessing. This will remain in my memory. I will treasure this last blessing that I got on my birthday. Then, three or four days later when I wanted a statement from her about Princess Diana, she gave me one. It appeared in my book about Princess Diana.

NEWSDAY: When did you publish your book about Princess Diana?

SRI CHINMOY: A few days ago. I had an interview with her on the 21st of May—just three months before she died. Then she wrote me two letters in June, three letters in the month of July and her last letter on the 7th of August—not even a month before she left the body.

NEWSDAY: This is amazing!

SRI CHINMOY: Her last letter mentions *Newsday*. Your newspaper said she was the Queen of American hearts, so I sent her a copy of the *Newsday* clipping. Also, I was grateful to be an instrument in arranging her last interview with Mother Teresa. She first met with Mother in 1992 in Rome. This year she wanted to meet her again, but she was unable to track her down. So I said that I would be responsible for making arrangements because I was going to have an interview with Mother. When I told Mother Teresa on the phone that Princess Diana wanted to see her, Mother said, "Tell her to come to New York." But Princess Diana wanted to see Mother in Europe. Then Mother Teresa was joking with me, saying, "If she does not want to come to New York to see me, then tell her to come and see me in Calcutta." So I wrote to the Princess and gave her Mother Teresa's phone number and address in the Bronx. Then she phoned up Mother and finally saw her.

NEWSDAY: That is amazing, amazing! God seems to have put you in the position to touch these two people's lives.

SRI CHINMOY: It is not that I touched their lives but that I was given a golden opportunity to be of service to them. God wanted Princess Diana to bring her spiritual dimension to the fore. Princess Diana had so many good qualities, but her prayer-life had not come to the fore. She did so much work for charity, for the poor, for the sick; but she also had another aspect, a spiritual aspect. That is why she wanted to see Mother Teresa and why she invited me to come and see her at Kensington Palace. Otherwise, she could have said, "Oh, I do not care for spiritual people." But her heart cried for God's Love and Light, the Light that Mother Teresa saw and served in Jesus Christ.

This same higher power made it possible for Princess Diana and I to meet just before her passing. For years I had wanted to meet her, without success. How did I succeed at the eleventh hour? It is because of the intercession of a higher power. And with Mother

Teresa also I developed such a close connection in the last few years of her life. I first met her in 1975, but many years passed before I saw her again. It is because at that time it was not necessary. But when God's choice Hour struck, we became closer than the closest.

And with Princess Diana, if I had not had that first and last interview, we never would have gotten to know one another. Plus these letters! How could one imagine that she would write on the 7th of August and three weeks later leave the earth-planet? After the 7th of August I doubt that many people received letters from her. And perhaps very few people had private interviews with her after the time I met her in May.

NEWSDAY: That's right, exactly! But apparently she was reaching out, too, in wanting to meet with you, and with Mother Teresa so soon afterwards.

SRI CHINMOY: Right! She was the one who asked me to make arrangements. She said, "I cannot track Mother Teresa down." I said, "I will do it." So I did it. I was the instrument, but her heart wanted to have the meeting. Otherwise, when I said to her that Mother Teresa is so kind and affectionate to me, she could have said, "Yes, yes, I am also an admirer of hers." But why did she say, "I want to meet with her. Can you tell me how I can meet with her?" She could have stopped at saying, "Yes, yes, I have deep admiration for her," but she was so eager to meet with her. Something inside Princess Diana was prompting her.

NEWSDAY: What a wonderful thing! Just in time!

SRI CHINMOY: She met with her in the middle of June. Then, within a few months both were gone. So you can say that their meeting was all God-ordained. When we pray and meditate, God does everything for us.

NEWSDAY: That's just simply amazing. You are so right. When you tune into a higher power, things happen.

SRI CHINMOY: The higher powers do it for us because we are their children. Children know nothing. Parents know what will give the children joy, so the parents do it. Children only know how to cry. The rest is done by the parents.

NEWSDAY: This has been really wonderful! Just absolutely wonderful! Will you be here for the rest of this week, or will you be travelling again soon?

SRI CHINMOY: I have just returned from Oslo and Warsaw. I was giving Peace Concerts there. I dedicated the Oslo concert to Princess Diana and the Warsaw concert to Mother Teresa. On the stage at Warsaw we had huge pictures of Mother Teresa.

NEWSDAY: Mother Teresa brings together both the spiritual life and the life of service.

SRI CHINMOY: She was a woman of prayer plus service. Mother Teresa always said, "Pray for me, pray for me, pray for me." In her, God wanted to unite service and prayer. In Diana's case, she was a woman of service—service to mankind. In my case, I pray and meditate first, and I also serve. I have been to so many countries offering Peace Concerts. Mother Teresa also did both. Every day she prayed and, at the same time, she served.

Princess Diana was young; she did not get the time or opportunity to enter into the prayer-life. That is why she did not take the prayer-life so seriously. But the service-life she did take seriously. At every moment she went here and there—to Angola, to Yugoslavia, to Pakistan and other places. She took the service-life more seriously, whereas Mother Teresa took both prayer and service seriously.

NEWSDAY: I am really happy that I made an effort to come, because this is far more than I expected. I think that we have touched on an aspect that nobody else has really dealt with—the connection between the three of you. It's amazing.

SRI CHINMOY: God brought us together. Mother Teresa was at the end of her life and Diana was at the prime of her life. I came in between, like a devoted bridge between the two.

NEWSDAY: You brought them together. That is more fascinating than the mind can even encompass.

SRI CHINMOY: The mind can never comprehend the inner realities. The mind is very limited; it is only a collector of information. With our mind we have read many books and talked to so many people on earth; but we have only collected information. Real knowledge and wisdom come from prayer and meditation—not from books. Otherwise, the professors and teachers would have been ruling the world. But they would have only misguided us. The more we remain in the mind, the more we are misguided. But if we can live in the heart, we are lifted up.

When we are in the mind, it is like being encaged; all the windows and doors are closed and we cannot go beyond it. It is like a prison cell, and we want to come out of it. But when we are in the heart, it is like being outside in a beautiful garden. So it is up to us. We can live in our own mind-prison, which we have created; and again, we can live in our own heart-garden, which is also our creation. If we are in the mind, the prison cell welcomes us; if we are in the heart, the garden welcomes us.

NEWSDAY: That's right. Exactly! Sri Chinmoy, I cannot tell you how happy I am now that we had this conversation.

SRI CHINMOY: We are sailing in the same boat. So many reporters have come, but they have not opened their hearts so beautifully and spiritually the way you have done. With one hand we cannot clap. Two hands are needed.

Let me autograph this book for you. *(Sri Chinmoy signs his book about Princess Diana and draws seven birds.)* Seven is for the seven higher worlds. There are seven higher worlds. When I die, when you die, we shall have to go to the seven higher worlds.

NEWSDAY: And I was born in the seventh month, too. This is wonderful. Thank you. Thanks are not enough. You know how I feel. I appreciate this.

SRI CHINMOY: Everything happens at God's choice Hour. These things could not have taken place if God's Hour had not struck. One was in Calcutta, one was in England and one was here in New York. See how God united us because of our love for Him. If we love God, then God brings everything together.

NEWSDAY: I believe that, I really do. This is why I am here.

Ms. Merle English of Newsday interviews Sri Chinmoy at Annam Brahma restaurant in Jamaica, Queens. Her full-page article appeared in the 'Queens Life' section of the Sunday edition on September 28th.

Newsday
SUNDAY, SEPTEMBER 28, 1997

A Coming Together of Luminaries

Diana's dream to meet Mother Teresa fulfilled with help of peace advocate

BY MERLE ENGLISH
STAFF WRITER

PRINCESS DIANA DIED last month having realized one of her fondest wishes. On June 18, at the Missionaries of Charity House in the South Bronx, she met Mother Teresa.

Briarwood resident and international peace advocate Sri Chinmoy helped Diana fulfill that wish.

While in London to perform at the Royal Albert Hall on May 21 — one of the 500 peace concerts he's given in 43 countries — Sri Chinmoy was invited to visit the princess at Kensington Palace just a few hours before she was to fly to Pakistan to visit children stricken with cancer.

Diana had been invited to the concert but couldn't attend because of her planned trip. But she received Sri Chinmoy, 66, in an interview room, meditated and prayed with him and listened to him sing — including songs in his native Bengali that he wrote for her and her two boys, William and Harry.

Accompanying himself on a keyboard, Sri Chinmoy also sang songs he composed from public statements Diana made, among them, "I am not a political figure," and, "Everyone needs to be valued." He said the songs moved her to comment, "I'm glad somebody listens to what I say."

His experiences with the two world figures are documented in two books he wrote and published this year: "Diana, Princess of Wales, Empress of the World," about his Kensington Palace visit with Diana, and, "Mother Teresa: Humanity's Flower-Heart, Divinity's Fragrance-Soul," a tribute that was also a birthday gift to the Nobel Peace Prize-winning nun.

Sri Chinmoy first met Mother Teresa in 1975 at a concert at the United Nations and they stayed in touch over the ensuing years. He recalled how at a meeting with her in Rome, in keeping with Indian tradition, as a gesture of respect he took off his sandals before entering the room where they were to talk. Mother Teresa told him if he didn't put his sandals back on she would have to remove hers, which she'd kept on because the room was cold.

He also remembered that she massaged his fingers and hands as a mother or an older sister would.

Sri Chinmoy had a private audience with the nun the day before she met the princess in New York, and on Aug. 26, just days before she died, Mother Teresa gave him a birthday blessing over the telephone, he said. A few days later, at his request, she sent him a statement on Diana's death that appears in his book about the princess, a limited edition that he said was for friends.

Sri Chinmoy and Princess Diana outside Kensington Palace in May
Photo by Bhavani Torti

QUEENS Diary

Diana accepted a special drawing of Sri Chinmoy's "Dream-Freedom-Peace-Birds" — he's done 7 million — that he made for her. When she recognized the letters "W", and "H" in the line drawing of two birds floating high amid puffy white clouds against an aquamarine sky, Sri Chinmoy said the princess exclaimed, "My boys, my boys!"

As they conversed, Sri Chinmoy mentioned to Diana that Mother Teresa was very fond of her and viewed her as a daughter. Diana told him she wanted to see the renowned nun but hadn't yet been able to.

"I said that I would be responsible for making arrangements because I was going to have an interview with Mother," Sri Chinmoy said he told her.

"I told Mother on the phone that Princess Diana would like to meet with her," He said Mother Teresa responded, "Tell her to come to New York."

"So I wrote the princess and gave her Mother Teresa's phone number and address in the Bronx. Then she phoned up Mother and finally saw her. I was the instrument, but her heart wanted to have the meeting."

Sri Chinmoy was one of Diana's longtime admirers.

"For years I wanted to meet with her because I had the deepest admiration for her philanthropy and charity and sincere compassion for the sick and suffering people," the musician, artist, athlete and author of close to 2,000 books said recently. He was sharing some of his recollections of the princess and Mother Teresa at the Annam Brahma vegetarian restaurant in Briarwood.

His communication with Diana began some months before they met.

He and students affiliated with his Sri Chinmoy International Center, headquartered in Jamaica, cut out and sent her positive newspaper and magazine stories about her to offset some of the negative press she received. He was one of the last people with whom Diana corresponded.

In letters he received from her dated July 21 and Aug. 7, Diana thanked him for sending her stories Newsday published about her, including an editorial headlined "Diana Has Found a Home in Americans' Hearts."

"I am still mourning my supreme loss," he said. "She was so kind and compassionate to me."

Sri Chinmoy recalled that the princess posed with him for photographs. She took one standing next to a table with a rare crystal sculpture of the Indian elephant god Ganesh.

"He's the one who gives us the fulfillment of our desires, provided our desires are sincere," he told her.

He told her she and Mother Teresa were sailing in the same boat, and the princess replied, "But I am a very, very small Mother Teresa."

When he was leaving the palace, Sri Chinmoy said, Princess Diana insisted on carrying his briefcase to a taxi she had called and paid for in advance.

He believes Diana died unhappy.

"The whole world can hate me, but I have to say that she was unhappy. Outwardly she was achieving something, but inwardly she was very, very unhappy," he said. "When people fall in love outwardly they can mix with their boyfriends and girlfriends, but inwardly they may feel miserable about what they are doing for many reasons . . . In Diana's case, outwardly we see she was mixing with this person and that person, that she was enjoying a holiday and so on, but inside, nobody knows what was happening."

He believes, however, that spiritually, the princess was growing.

"If Princess Diana did not believe in the inner life she would not have admired and adored Mother Teresa," he said. "She would not have asked me to come and see her . . . But she did have a hunger for spirituality. That hunger compelled her to make time to see me."

"So my personal feeling is that outwardly, although she was sometimes leading a kind of glamorous and romantic life, inwardly she did not really want that. Inwardly, she wanted to have a peaceful life. Spirituality was beginning to bud and bloom in the princess, only it did not have an opportunity to blossom the way her service-life had already blossomed." •

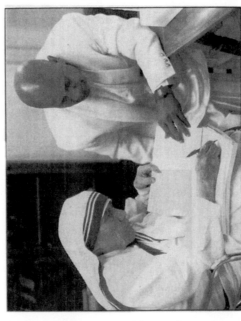

Sri Chinmoy and Mother Teresa at the Missionaries of Charity House in the South Bronx

Photo by Dhano Alalmo

Sri Chinmoy
prepares for a series
of live radio interviews
on September 25th.

A powerful moment between two God-lovers as Monsignor Thomas Hartman, known affectionately to his friends as Father Tom, welcomes Sri Chinmoy to the studio of Telecare Cablevision of Rockville Centre, Long Island.

In the library of the Telecare studio, prior to the interview, Sri Chinmoy and Father Tom share their experiences of Mother Teresa, and Sri Chinmoy reads Father Tom his eulogy for Mother Teresa.

"Joining me to talk about this very special saint, the saint of the gutters, the saint of our times, Mother Teresa, is my good friend Sri Chinmoy." With these words, Father Tom begins his special half-hour programme dedicated to Mother Teresa. Both Father Tom and Sri Chinmoy were personal friends of Mother Teresa and Father Tom offered the live commentary for her funeral service on Channel 55, Long Island.

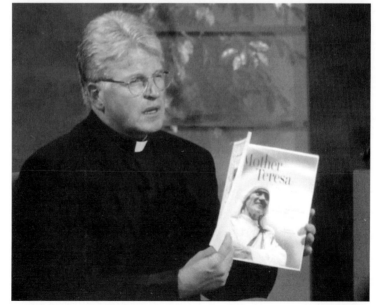

Sri Chinmoy is interviewed about his friendship with Mother Teresa on Cablevision 12, New Jersey.

QUESTIONS AND ANSWERS ABOUT MOTHER TERESA

On 10 September Sri Chinmoy answered the following questions from his students about Mother Teresa.

QUESTION: How can we develop the love for God's creation that Mother Teresa had?

SRI CHINMOY: Right now name and form are creating problems for us and separating us from one another. I have one name; someone else has a different name. But if we can go beyond name and form, we discover that there is only one Name, and that is God.

There are many ways to love God the creation, but humility is of paramount importance. If we have humility, then nothing is beneath our dignity; there is nothing that we shall not do for our expanded selves. Mother Teresa's humility is genuine, but in the case of most people it is false. While we are touching the feet of someone, we feel that the whole world is appreciating, admiring and adoring us for our humility. Our body is at the feet of the other person, but our mind is somewhere else—on the top of the Himalayas.

In genuine humility, when we touch someone's feet, at that time we place our entire existence—body, vital, mind, heart and soul—

at that person's feet. We feel that everything we have and everything we are is at the person's feet. When a disciple falls at the feet of his spiritual Master, his very breath must touch the Master's feet and enter into the Master's heart of compassion. At that time the Master does not feel superior. No, he only feels his oneness with the disciple.

Mother Teresa's whole vision and mission were founded on humility. If she had not had humility in boundless measure, she would not have gone out into the streets of Calcutta. She went out into the streets of Calcutta and made her home in the slums because she felt her inseparable oneness with the suffering life and bleeding heart of humanity. When we have humility, automatically we increase our love of God the creation.

QUESTION: Mother Teresa's path was very austere. I am wondering whether that austerity was needed for her to be so successful with her charity work.

SRI CHINMOY: From the highest spiritual point of view, austerity is not needed. Austerity is like self-mortification. God does not ask us to mortify ourselves in order to come close to Him; it is not necessary to do so. But again, Mother Teresa's view of what constitutes austerity and our view of what constitutes austerity may be totally different. According to our standard, we may call her life austere, but she will use the term 'natural'. We say, "You do not see movies. You do not wear nice clothes and eat good food. You deny even the basic necessities in your life." But she will say, "I do not take these things as basic necessities. To me, they are extravagant; they are unimportant." For her, wearing simple clothes and eating the same kind of food for months and months is natural. For us it may seem austere, but she will say, "No, that way of life has become natural for me." So who is to judge what is natural and what is unnatural? If, by following her way of life, which is natural to her, she is making the fastest progress, who are we to criticise her?

Similarly, we can be criticised for leading a pleasure-life. In my case, because of my knee pain, I am getting massaged. Somebody may say, "What is he doing? Like a king or emperor he is getting massaged two or three times a day!" But for me this knee massage is absolutely necessary so that I can get joy from walking a little. If people who are leading more austere lives want to find fault with me, easily they can. But if getting massaged and taking Western vitamins is not lowering my consciousness, if I am not descending by doing this, then I feel it is perfectly all right. In Mother Teresa's case also, if she was not torturing her body or lowering her consciousness by leading an austere life, if she was making progress, then there is nothing wrong with that lifestyle.

We may say that austerity is not needed to realise God. We can utilise modern conveniences and so forth. Mother Teresa and her Sisters, on the other hand, will say that modern conveniences are an extra coat that they have to carry on their journey. Whatever point of view you follow, the most important thing is to make the fastest progress. If someone can make fastest progress on the strength of his or her austerity, fine! And if I can make the fastest progress by following a different lifestyle, then I will do that. I know my way is not the only way. I cannot say that there is no other way to realise God. No, my way is suitable for me, and another way is suitable for someone else. If we are each arriving at the goal by following our own way, then only a fool would criticise us, for our sole aim is to arrive at the destination.

There are many paths. By caring for lepers and people with AIDS and other illnesses, Mother Teresa's Sisters are doing the right thing. Again, our way is to pray to God most sincerely to cure the sick. One approach is the way of service, and the other is the way of prayer. We cannot say that their way is wrong, and they cannot say that our way is wrong.

QUESTION: It seems that Mother Teresa's mission or path is similar to that of Saint Francis. Is there any connection?

SRI CHINMOY: You can say that the mission is similar, but she did not come into the world as a complementary soul to Saint Francis. They both travelled in the same type of boat, but there was no direct connection between their souls.

Saint Francis was guided and inspired by the Saviour Christ to walk along one particular road. Again, the Saviour Christ took Mother Teresa along the same road. But she did not get the inspiration or aspiration from her predecessor. Like Saint Francis, she received everything directly from the Saviour Christ. He was her only inspiration. Quite often she used the word 'Jesus' rather than 'Christ'. Jesus and the Christ are the same, but she uses the term 'Jesus' more. So if anybody inspired her or aspired through her for the manifestation of God's Light, then it was Jesus Christ.

QUESTION: Was the timing of Mother Teresa's passing meant to help Princess Diana enter into the higher worlds?

SRI CHINMOY: Mother Teresa's passing has no direct connection with Princess Diana's passing. At God's choice Hour, His destined Hour, Mother Teresa left us. Mother Teresa did not go just because Princess Diana needed help. Princess Diana's soul is very beautiful and very developed, but in terms of spiritual maturity, Mother Teresa's soul is infinitely higher. In the soul's world Mother Teresa will gladly be of blessingful service to Princess Diana's soul. Mother Teresa's compassion, affection, light and other divine qualities will definitely help Princess Diana, but not immediately. It may take a few months or even a few years.

Both of them are now in totally different planes of consciousness. Mother Teresa is being worshipped and adored by angels, archangels and other divine beings. She is in one world, Diana is in another world, which is also extremely beautiful, and Sri Chinmoy is crying and dancing, dancing and crying, somewhere else.

QUESTION: Mother Teresa taught us many beautiful lessons through her example, but I never could comprehend what she meant when she talked about the beauty she saw in dying people.

SRI CHINMOY: It is one thing to theoretically say, "God is inside everybody; that is why I love you." But it is another thing to say, "I see you as God Himself." In dying people Mother Teresa saw the living presence of Jesus Christ. Her oneness with God the creation was so unique or, you can say, so perfect that she did not see the dying person as an ordinary human being. She saw the dying person as Jesus Christ Himself. She was not seeing Jesus Christ *inside* the dying person; she was seeing the dying person as Jesus Christ Himself. This is the experience that Jesus Christ gave her because He was so pleased with her. This is a unique experience that she had, which she was sharing with us.

QUESTION: Did Mother Teresa's dynamism come from the vital, or did it come from her soul's conviction?

SRI CHINMOY: It was her soul's conviction that she was able to manifest in her heart. Then, from her heart she brought it into her entire life. We say that the pure vital dynamism is of paramount importance for divine manifestation, which is true. But her dynamism came from her soul, which is even better, and from there it went into her heart and then into her life. Hers was the dynamism of the heart, not of the vital. You can say it was the illumination of her soul that was transferred first into her heart and then into her life proper. When it entered into her heart, it was dynamism; but when it entered into her life, it became sympathy or compassion. In the soul's world it was illumination; in the heart it became dynamism and in the physical body, it became sympathy. Illumination has these two additional names. In her heart it became dynamism, and in her physical, earthly life it became sympathy or compassion.

QUESTION: Was it destiny or coincidence that Mother Teresa began her mission and spent so many years in India?

SRI CHINMOY: She came into the world with abundant light, and her soul was destined to play that role. So how can this be a coincidence? When she first went to India, she was teaching geography. But God was only waiting for the right moment. At His choice Hour, He entered into her own mother and awakened her.

Then her mother reminded her, "You went to India to serve the poor, not to teach geography." Mother Teresa was destined to play that inimitable role; it was not coincidence.

QUESTION: When I saw the video of your first meeting with Mother Teresa in Rome, Mother Teresa's voice rang like a bell. I was wondering if you could comment on the special quality in her voice.

SRI CHINMOY: Each time she speaks, her inner being rings the bell of the divine Victory of the Saviour Jesus Christ. Outwardly you can hear her speaking English or some other language; it is melodious. But inwardly her soul is ringing the Victory-bell for Jesus Christ.

"NEW JERSEY TALKING"
CABLEVISION 12, NEW JERSEY
12 SEPTEMBER 1997

INTERVIEWER: MS. PAGE HOPKINS

INTERVIEWER: Tonight on our show we'll meet one of Mother Teresa's friends. He'll talk to us about her life, her memory and his mission for peace.

Our guest is Sri Chinmoy. He was a friend of Mother Teresa's for over 20 years, and he spoke with her just nine days before her death. He's also the author of a book about the late nun, and he's here now to share his memories of her with us. Welcome!

This was such a tremendous loss to the world. Were you surprised by her death?

SRI CHINMOY: I was shocked beyond my imagination. When I asked her about her health only nine days before her final departure, she said to me, "Sri Chinmoy, I am much better, much better. Pray for me as I pray for you every day."

I met with her five times. The first time was in 1975 at the United Nations during an interfaith programme sponsored by the Temple of Understanding. They wanted me to offer a meditation at the beginning of the programme and then offer roses to all the religious leaders.

INTERVIEWER: What was your impression when you met her? Did she just radiate?

SRI CHINMOY: Simplicity, purity, humility: these three virtues are of paramount importance, and these are what I noticed and felt the moment I prayerfully stood in front of her with my rose.

INTERVIEWER: There's been such a rush in the last week to canonise her, and there's been a lot of talk of the Vatican waiving the preliminary five years. Do you think that was so important to her?

SRI CHINMOY: Nothing is important to her, but it is important for humanity. Sometimes it happens that when we honour someone, the person who is being honoured does not need it or care for it. But while we are honouring that person we increase our own inspiration and aspiration to become better citizens of the world. While appreciating, admiring and adoring the other person, we increase our own capacities and bring to the fore our own divine potential.

INTERVIEWER: The timing of her death is also interesting—coming in the wake of the very public death of Princess Diana, which the world really has been so obsessed with. In terms of media coverage, maybe Mother Teresa's death would have even been a bigger deal had it not been eclipsed by Princess Diana's. Do you think that's the way she would have wanted it?

SRI CHINMOY: Princess Diana at times wanted media and at times she did not. When she was doing something for the betterment of the world, when she was doing charity work and meeting with the sick and poor, she wanted media attention in order to uplift the consciousness of the world. But sometimes the media exposed her frailties and weaknesses, which we all have, and at that time she did not welcome the media attention. She said that this kind of thing does not help humanity in any way. She wanted only to inspire the rest of the world, but unfortunately the media always tries to find the negative side of things. That is a very painful experience. Everything has its darker side and its brighter side. But if you weigh the pros and cons of her life, her good qualities and virtues will far surpass her so-called human weaknesses.

INTERVIEWER: Unfortunately, the media tend to accentuate the more frivolous aspects of her life. What was your impression of Princess Diana as a person when you met her?

SRI CHINMOY: Very kind, very compassionate and, at the same time, very self-giving! I was the instrument in helping Princess Diana to meet with Mother Teresa in June this year in New York. I told her how she could be in touch with Mother Teresa. I am so happy and grateful that I was able to serve both luminaries at the same time.

INTERVIEWER: Did these two women, as the press has said, have a lot in common?

SRI CHINMOY: It was right from my childhood. At the age of four I started praying, and when I was seven years old I started praying and meditating consciously and seriously. At the age of 32 I was invited by some American seekers to come to the West and be of service to America. Since then, I have been offering prayers and meditations at the United Nations and I have offered over 500 prayerful Peace Concerts in various countries. I have also written many, many books.

I feel that world peace can come into being on the strength of our prayer and meditation. This is my way. Many roads lead to Rome, but I prefer this particular road. It is my personal opinion and inmost conviction that it is through prayer and meditation that we shall be able to bring about world peace.

INTERVIEWER: Do you believe the world is becoming a more peaceful place?

SRI CHINMOY: Yes, I feel so. There was a time when people did not believe in a peaceful existence. There was the First World War and the Second World War. A Third World War was threatening, but fortunately it did not take place. Then the politicians started talking about peace. For most of this century it was not so widely practised. Now talking has surrendered to acting. I feel that there are quite a few politicians in the world today who believe in peace, and who most sincerely try to bring about world peace. Peace is no longer just a dictionary word; it is becoming a living reality. It may take time, but we are walking along the right road.

INTERVIEWER: Many people working in news feel powerless when they read stories about religious wars in Bosnia or Ireland. And peace is virtually hanging in the balance in the Middle East. It makes you wonder what you can possibly do to make a difference.

SRI CHINMOY: Pray! There is no other way. We cannot change the minds of others by exercising our mental power or military power or any other kind of power. We can only change their minds through prayer. The greatest, most effective prayer is: "Let Thy Will be done." This prayer we have received from the Saviour Christ. If we can consciously identify ourself with the Will of God, then there is bound to come a time when this world of ours will be inundated with peace. We have tried and will continue to try many other processes, but I feel it is by virtue of prayer that one day our world will have true, genuine peace.

INTERVIEWER: And Thy Will be done—invoking God's Will. Well, this has been very inspirational. Thank you so much for coming by and sharing your memories of Mother Teresa and Princess Diana with us—two women who really touched this world in a way that will reverberate for many centuries to come.

SRI CHINMOY: Definitely!

TELECARE CABLE TELEVISION
ROCKVILLE CENTRE, LONG ISLAND
15 SEPTEMBER 1997

HOST: MONSIGNOR THOMAS HARTMAN
(FATHER TOM)

Introductory music: a tape of the Sri Chinmoy Bhajan Singers performing the song "Mother Teresa: Humanity's Flower-Heart, Divinity's Fragrance-Soul."

FATHER TOM: I'm Father Tom. Gerard Manley Hopkins once said that "the earth is touched by the grandeur of God," and I believe that. Walk outside; look at the sky, look at the plants, look at the animal creation, look at the extent of the Universe. But especially look at people. We're all touched by God—given a soul, a character, spirituality. We have so many capacities to love and to care, to make this a better world. But it seems to me that those who actualise it the most are people of prayer, people who recognise that they need to work on their spirituality, people who learn how to be silent, people of faith, people of love and people of service.

I was blown away, as everyone was, in the week that both Princess Di and Mother Teresa died. I'd like to focus in on a very special relationship that our guest enjoyed with Mother Teresa. It's true that Princess Di did many extraordinary things in her life—her humanity, her struggles, her willingness to break out of very tight

Telecare Cable Television
Rockville Centre, Long Island
15 September 1997

Host: Monsignor Thomas Hartman
(Father Tom)

Introductory music: a tape of the Sri Chinmoy Bhajan Singers performing the song "Mother Teresa: Humanity's Flower-Heart, Divinity's Fragrance-Soul."

FATHER TOM: I'm Father Tom. Gerard Manley Hopkins once said that "the earth is touched by the grandeur of God," and I believe that. Walk outside; look at the sky, look at the plants, look at the animal creation, look at the extent of the Universe. But especially look at people. We're all touched by God—given a soul, a character, spirituality. We have so many capacities to love and to care, to make this a better world. But it seems to me that those who actualise it the most are people of prayer, people who recognise that they need to work on their spirituality, people who learn how to be silent, people of faith, people of love and people of service.

I was blown away, as everyone was, in the week that both Princess Di and Mother Teresa died. I'd like to focus in on a very special relationship that our guest enjoyed with Mother Teresa. It's true that Princess Di did many extraordinary things in her life—her humanity, her struggles, her willingness to break out of very tight confines, saying she wanted her kids to learn how to sing, her willingness to cheerfully touch an HIV person. She did not remove herself from the human story. She wanted to be a part of that. While she did that, her celebrity or her sanctity needed to touch base with *the* saint of our times, Mother Teresa.

Mother Teresa! This is her business card: "The fruit of silence is prayer. The fruit of prayer is faith. The fruit of faith is love. The fruit of love is service. The fruit of service is peace." She literally embraced a way of life in Calcutta in which she would go to the gutters and pick up a person with maggots, clutch that person to her breast, bring that person to her convent, take out the maggots, wash the person down, put them in new clothes. This saint of the gutters touched all of our lives. At her funeral when different people from different religions came and spoke about her, they said, "She is the saint of the world." How proud I was of her! The grandeur of God certainly was revealed through her.

Joining me to talk about this very special saint, the saint of the gutters, the saint of our times, Mother Teresa, is my good friend Sri Chinmoy, spiritual leader of Sri Chinmoy: The Peace Meditation at the United Nations and a mentor to me and to so many others. Sri Chinmoy, when you think of Mother Teresa—you met her, you talked with her—what comes to your mind?

SRI CHINMOY: Her compassion and her universal heart! She was the Mother of infinite compassion and she was, is and forever will remain a universal heart.

FATHER TOM: There's a picture of her holding a one-pound ten-ounce child, saying that she and her Sisters want to live in such a way that before this child died, it would get a hug. Once I walked with her around the South Bronx. When the homeless people saw her pick up a child who had a contagious disease, they said they knew she had heart. Many of us know those pictures and know the stories. Can you tell me a little bit about how a person begins in the spiritual life, how a person like her got to the point where she was so one with creation?

SRI CHINMOY: She was destined to be a supremely chosen child of the Saviour Christ. She not only saw or felt in each individual the presence of the Saviour Christ, but she actually took each individual as the living embodiment of the Saviour Christ. When somebody was dying, in that person she saw the compassionate face of the living Christ. It was unimaginable! To her, each individual was the Saviour Christ.

She served the poor and the needy with the feeling that she was ordained to perform this supreme task. She was doing this not for the sake of any individual; she was doing this for her own highest Source. She saw her Source inside the other individual and felt the other individual as her Source itself. Whenever she helped someone, she was loving and serving the Christ and nobody else. So her compassion was unique. Her oneness with the compassion and forgiveness of the Saviour Christ and Mother Mary will not have any equal on earth.

FATHER TOM: There is a passage in Matthew's Gospel which says, "Jesus at the end of time will gather everyone before Him and He'll say, 'I was hungry, and you fed Me. I was thirsty, and you gave Me drink. I was in prison, and you visited Me. You did it to Me.'"

MY MOTHER OF COMPASSION, MY SISTER OF AFFECTION

Mother Teresa would say, "If you want to know what the Gospel is about, that's what it is about: You did it to Me." In other words, she prayed that her eyes could see the Presence of God in each person. Sri Chinmoy had the privilege, as I had, of meeting with Mother Teresa shortly before she died. Members of his community went to see her. We now have a tape of Mother Teresa meeting with Sri Chinmoy.

A video tape is shown of Sri Chinmoy and his students meeting with Mother Teresa.

FATHER TOM: This woman, this saint, 87 years old, with all sorts of medical conditions, exposed to all sorts of diseases in the world, just went forward. Twelve years ago I remember she talked with me about coming back from seeing Fidel Castro. She said to him, "Fidel, you are such a good boy. Don't you think it is time to come back?" And then she talked at that time about opening up convents in the Soviet Union, and she managed not just to open up one but actually four convents. But most recently, at age 87, she was talking about China, and I know the two of you talked about that. She really wanted to get to China.

SRI CHINMOY: She really wanted to have something in China. She told me at least six times that she wanted me to accompany her to China. She said, "China needs light. China needs light." I am sure the Absolute Lord Supreme from Heaven will fulfil her desire through her Sisters.

FATHER TOM: So the first lesson we learn is that she was able to see God's Life in each person. She didn't see the leprosy; she saw the Life of God. She used to say that she was a pencil in the Hand of God. She was an instrument to be used by God. You are suggesting that she is saying that we are called to introduce the Light of God into circumstances where there may be darkness.

SRI CHINMOY: She tried to illumine darkness on the strength of her compassion, on the strength of her oneness. She felt that we have to come down to the level of the ones we are serving. If someone is poor, then we have to renounce our wealth and live at the poverty level with them. She felt that the richer we are, the more complaints we have. According to her, poor people do not complain; they just suffer. And it is God who is experiencing suffering in and through them. They are not aware of it, but Mother Teresa was fully aware of it.

If we do not make complaints, we go forward. We see the better side of life, the purer side of life. By seeing the better and purer side of life even in the midst of direst poverty, she was able to derive tremendous satisfaction from what she was doing. She received satisfaction not only because she was seeing the living presence of Jesus Christ in those she served, but also because they were so receptive to what she was trying to offer. With utmost gratitude they were receiving the light that she was bringing down from Above.

FATHER TOM: When she first moved into the Bronx, the convent that she embraced was in a very difficult section of the Bronx. There's a lot of poverty, a lot of drugs, a lot of homelessness, a lot of hunger. One of the first things she did was have them take the beds out. The Sisters slept on the floor. She did not want her Sisters to have any privilege that the poorest person in the community did not have. And she went on to say, "How can I say to the poor that I understand them and love them when I live differently than they?" Each of her Sisters had two saris and a bucket.

You are indicating that sometimes the richer we are, the more complaints we have. Is it necessary or is it advisable in the spiritual life that we do with less, that we have fewer possessions and maybe more heart?

SRI CHINMOY: Certainly! Each extra possession is an extra headache. In the outer life, the more we try to possess things that we do not need, the more problems we create for ourselves. The simpler the better! In the spiritual life, it is always good to find a shortcut to our destination. All roads lead to Rome, true, but there is a way to arrive in Rome that is faster than the other ways, and that way is the simplicity-road. The simpler we are, the quicker we can arrive at our destination.

FATHER TOM: David Suskind was once doing a documentary on Mother Teresa, and he was following her around for a week. At the end of the week, Joy Suskind, his wife, looked at Mother Teresa and said, "Mother, where do you get this energy? Where do you get this spirituality? Where do you find all of this joy?" Mother looked at her and said, "Would you like this energy?" Joy said, "Yes." So Mother said, "Receive the Eucharist."

Sri Chinmoy, you are a person of deep prayer. Those who are viewing us may be moved by Mother Teresa's death and may want to live more like Mother Teresa did. They may be inspired to embrace the life of prayer. So let me ask you, what is it that gives somebody energy, perspective, hope and love from prayer?

SRI CHINMOY: Prayer is everything. Prayer is our inseparable oneness with the Source. "Let Thy Will be done"—this is the highest prayer. No prayer can be compared with this prayer that the Saviour taught us. A tiny drop can maintain its own separate existence. Again, the same drop, if it is wise, will throw itself into the mighty ocean and become one with the infinite ocean. So this prayer—"Let Thy Will be done"— is the supreme secret that enables the finite not only to enter into the Infinite but to become the Infinite itself. I am an ordinary, insignificant human being, a tiny drop. But the moment I realise that God is my All and surrender what little I have to Him, the moment I lose my existence in God and become one with God, I become what He has and what He is. I have nothing, but if I can give that very nothingness to God cheerfully and unconditionally, then God will give me what He has and what He is. So prayer is the secret of secrets to become one with the Absolute Lord Supreme.

FATHER TOM: Mother Teresa certainly saw the tougher side of life. She saw people hungry, people dying, people diseased. And yet she had great joy. I think that many of us would get burned out and feel stressed in a similar situation. We might after a while become pretty negative about life. How could she maintain her poise and positive outlook?

SRI CHINMOY: Father, precisely because she did it not for herself but for her highest Self, which is all-pervading. If my leg needs something, my hand will not hesitate to do the needful because my hand knows that my leg is part and parcel of my body. Similarly, Mother Teresa did not have any sense of separativity; she took humanity as her own, very own. If I take somebody as my own, then I will not take my service-life to them as a sacrifice, but as my bounden duty.

FATHER TOM: She was not separated. She was connected to God and she was doing God's Work in the world.

SRI CHINMOY: She was doing God's Work, and also she felt that it was God who was acting in and through her. With His right Hand, God offered her the capacity to give, and with His left Hand, God offered her the capacity to receive. God in her was both the Giver and the Receiver. So God gave her the energy, light, compassion and all the other divine virtues that she needed to serve Him in the poor.

FATHER TOM: So she was opening up her soul to the Grace of God.

SRI CHINMOY: She was unfolding and blossoming. While she was blossoming, she became a fountain of affection, compassion and forgiveness.

FATHER TOM: And yet when she received the Nobel Prize, she said, "I am unworthy, but I receive this on behalf of those who are hungry and sick and poor."

SRI CHINMOY: They usually have a party to celebrate the Nobel laureates. In her case she said, "You give me the seven thousand or ten thousand dollars that you had planned to spend on the party, and I will use it for a better cause—for the poor."

FATHER TOM: She would go to somebody's house. They would offer her food. She would turn down the food, but as she was leaving she would say, "Could you make a doggy bag? I can bring this food to the poor." Extraordinary!

SRI CHINMOY: Sleeplessly and breathlessly she thought of the poor, but not in the sense of being superior. She saw them as part and parcel of her own existence. Her compassion, love, affection and blessings were for everybody. She was like the sun. The sun is for everybody. It is up to me to receive its light by keeping my doors and windows open.

FATHER TOM: Isn't that wonderful! This earth is really for everyone. We are all loved by God. You had the privilege of knowing her personally and talking with her. She is obviously a saint. When I went to see her, she looked at me and said, "Father, please pray for me." It was so humbling because here is a saint asking me to pray for her.

SRI CHINMOY: Forgive me to say, in my case she used to show her emotional aspect. With sisterly, motherly affection, she used to tell me, "I pray for you every day. You must pray for me." On the phone she would say, "Sri Chinmoy, I pray for you; you must pray for me." I met with her for the first time in 1975. The Temple of

Understanding sponsored a meeting at the United Nations with about twenty religious leaders. They asked me to offer a minute of silence and then to give roses to each religious leader. As soon as I stood in front of her, I saw and felt that she was simplicity, purity and humility incarnate. When I went to her, I felt like a drop merging into the ocean. This was the experience I had.

FATHER TOM: As great a person as she was, when you were in her presence, for me it was like being with my grandmother, who was saying the rosary. When I would see my grandmother, she would say, "What are you doing?" And I would say, "I have a test to study for." She would say, "I'll pray for you."

SRI CHINMOY: I had exactly the same experience—that she was like a grandmother. She was for us in every aspect of life, not only while we were in the seventh Heaven of delight but also while we were swimming in the sea of sorrows. She became inseparably one with us in all our day-to-day activities.

FATHER TOM: Sometimes in this world you are encouraged to be efficient and effective and all that. Mother Teresa stands out to remind us that we are called just to be faithful, just to be loving, just to be engaging, to see the presence of God in every aspect. She attained happiness. She attained sanctity. What a model for us! She took the words in the Bible and put them into her heart and lived those words.

SRI CHINMOY: That is absolutely true. She did not want us to be self-sufficient. She wanted us to be God-efficient, that is to say, to depend upon God's Compassion, Love and Forgiveness. No matter how hard we try on our own to become perfect human beings, it is impossible. It is only God's infinite Compassion and Forgiveness that can one day transform our nature and make us good citizens of the world. She taught us to depend entirely upon God and not upon our own capacity.

If we human beings have a little capacity in any field, we tend to extol ourselves to the skies. If we are sincere, we will see that our human capacity is next to nothing; it is useless. But if we depend upon God's Compassion and God's Forgiveness, then His infinite Capacity becomes our own. Mother Teresa always taught us to become one with God's Will and to make His Capacity our own, rather than to rely on our own physical, vital or mental power.

FATHER TOM: A number of Sri Chinmoy's students are now going to sing a song that Sri Chinmoy wrote about Mother Teresa, and we are going to have the privilege of listening to that song. After that, you will be able to hear the special prayer that Sri Chinmoy has written for Mother Teresa.

A video clip is shown of the Sri Chinmoy Bhajan Singers performing "My Morning-Evening-Prayer-Song."

FATHER TOM: People throughout the world, grateful for Mother Teresa, are offering prayers and songs on her behalf. This document contains a special prayer by Sri Chinmoy. Could you read your prayer?

MY MOTHER OF COMPASSION, MY SISTER OF AFFECTION

SRI CHINMOY:

Mother Teresa:
    Calcutta's Soaring Bird
    India's Sailing Moon
    The World's Weeping Sky
    Earth's Tearing Loss
    Heaven's Dancing Gain
    The Christ's Blossoming Promise
    The Mother Mary's Harvesting Pride

FATHER TOM: We have known a saint. We believe that she is with God. But even though she is dead, her cause continues—the cause of sanctity, the cause of caring for the poorest of the poor. Consider making a donation to the Missionaries of Charity on her behalf. They will need your help. God bless you.

To end the programme, the tape is played once more of the Sri Chinmoy Bhajan Singers singing "Mother Teresa: Humanity's Flower-Heart, Divinity's Fragrance-Soul."

"Real Talk"
Radio WLIB, New York
15 September 1997

Interviewer: Mark Riley

INTERVIEWER: Tell us if you can, Sir, how you saw Mother Teresa's impact, not just on the people that she helped but on others who might have been inspired to follow her lead in terms of looking to help the poor.

SRI CHINMOY: There is not a single human being on earth who wants to be a good citizen of the world who was not or is not inspired by her. Directly as well as indirectly, consciously as well as unconsciously, she has served humanity. Her approach was unique. She could come down to any level. She could mix with the poorer than the poorest as well as the richer than the richest. She could be with the mightier than the mightiest and the weaker than the weakest. She had a universal heart that could mix with all and sundry, irrespective of their height or status in society.

INTERVIEWER: Very, very true! Tell us, if you could, about what Mother Teresa's work was like in India. India being such a long way from the United States, many Americans simply saw in her an image of a nun trying to help poor people. But I'm not sure that folks are really aware of the impact of her work in India.

MY MOTHER OF COMPASSION, MY SISTER OF AFFECTION

SRI CHINMOY: In India she was at once the Mother of compassion and the Sister of affection. She became the very heart of India's poverty. The poor and the needy claimed her as their very own, and also she claimed these unimaginably suffering human beings as her own. It was a matter of inseparable oneness that she established with the Indians.

So India claimed her as its very own. That is why India gave her the kind of State funeral that was accorded only to Mahatma Gandhi, the Father of the Indian Nation. She got the same kind of honour.

IN THE STUDIO OF
SATELLITE CHANNEL: SEDAT 00
NEW YORK
24 SEPTEMBER 1997

Sri Chinmoy was interviewed separately by ABC News affiliates:

WIBC, Indianapolis (Live)
WABC News, New York
WJR, Detroit (Live)
WLW, Cincinnati (Live)
WGY, Albany (Aired September 25th)

Radio WIBC
Indianapolis

INTERVIEWER: Our next guest is a prolific author, a poet, an artist, a musician, an athlete, a spiritual guide. He has spent time with world leaders such as Pope Paul VI, Pope John Paul II, Mikhail Gorbachev, Nelson Mandela, Archbishop Desmond Tutu and Mother Teresa, just before she passed on. Sri Chinmoy is with us this morning.

Sir, how were you able to obtain access to world leaders like the ones I just mentioned, and of course Mother Teresa, too?

SRI CHINMOY: I am a student of peace, and I wanted to meet with them. They were extremely kind to me and they complied with my request. Afterwards, I became very close friends with some of them.

INTERVIEWER: I know you had been acquainted with Mother Teresa for quite a bit. What struck you about Mother Teresa the first time you ever met her?

SRI CHINMOY: When I met with her for the first time, I prayerfully offered her a rose, and she blessingfully accepted the rose from me. I saw in her humility, simplicity, affection and compassion in boundless measure. This meeting took place on 24 October 1975, at the United Nations.

INTERVIEWER: Why did you write a book about her?

SRI CHINMOY: I wrote a book entitled *Mother Teresa: Humanity's Flower-Heart, Divinity's Fragrance-Soul*. I had met with her four times, each time for 45 minutes or an hour or so. I was also blessed with quite a few letters from her, and I had the greatest opportunity to speak with her on the telephone a number of times. All these I wanted to be recorded. *Mother Teresa: Humanity's Flower-Heart, Divinity's Fragrance-Soul* contains all these things.

INTERVIEWER: Sri Chinmoy, a very interesting book on Mother Teresa. Nice having you on the programme this morning, and good luck to you!

WABC News
New York

INTERVIEWER: Let me begin by saying the book that you wrote is a beautiful tribute for Mother Teresa. I understand that you have met her on several occasions, and in fact that you share a birthday. Can you tell me a little bit about the last time you spoke with her?

SRI CHINMOY: My last conversation with her has been recorded. She was extremely kind to me as usual. She was both a sister and a mother to me. As a sister, she inundated me with affection. As a mother, she inundated me with compassion. Her affectionate demand was, "You must pray for me, as I pray for you every day."

Then she had something else to say: "You must come with me to China. China needs light." Five or six times over the years she has asked me to accompany her to China. When I met with her on the 3rd of June this year and on the 17th of June at the Missionaries of Charity in the Bronx, she said the same thing: "You must come with me to China. China needs light. China needs light." So I promised her, "Yes, Mother, when the time comes, when you go to China, I shall definitely accompany you."

INTERVIEWER: Obviously that trip never took place. Will you carry on her request to bring peace, love and compassion and her work to China?

SRI CHINMOY: I shall pray and meditate, and if I get a command from within, if it is the Will of God, then definitely I shall go. But otherwise, I am not entitled to act on her behalf. I am a man of prayer. I was very, very closely connected to Mother Teresa, but it is for Sister Nirmala, who is Mother Teresa's successor and representative, to carry on her work. It is she who has to go to China and do the needful. I am a great admirer, a sincere admirer, of Mother Teresa. I promised her that I shall help the Missionaries of Charity according to my very limited capacity. I have students who are in the medical field, and they are able to offer the Missionaries of Charity medical supplies which have been donated by large companies. Also, in various other capacities whenever the Sisters need any help from me, I shall gladly do it.

INTERVIEWER: What do you see for the Missionaries of Charity now that Mother Teresa has passed away? Is there anyone who is with us now in the world who can even compare with her?

SRI CHINMOY: Nobody can be compared with her. She is matchless; she is unique. But her successor, Sister Nirmala, will be receiving blessings and guidance from Above—from Mother Teresa's soul in Heaven. Mother Teresa will be able to guide Sister Nirmala at every step. I know both of them well, so I know the daughter will always get inner guidance and special blessings from Mother, and she will be able to carry on Mother's mission. I have implicit faith in Mother's capacity and also I have implicit faith in Sister Nirmala's receptivity. Nirmala cannot be compared with Mother Teresa, true, but Mother Teresa will successfully be able to fulfil her mission in and through Sister Nirmala.

INTERVIEWER: You've met some very spiritual people in your life, obviously Mother Teresa being one of them. You've also met Pope John Paul. Can you compare the levels of spirituality in these great people and their works?

SRI CHINMOY: Each one has a special role to play on earth. They cannot be compared. Each human being is unique in his own way. Let us take the Holy Father. I have met with him on five occasions. Each time, he has blessed me most affectionately and most compassionately. To me, the Holy Father is our universal grandfather. No matter what we do, he is ready to shower his choicest compassion, protection and forgiveness upon us. In a family, children may do quite a few wrong things. Their parents may be annoyed, but their grandparents are always ready to forgive them. The Holy Father is like that; he is all compassion and forgiveness. No matter what we do, he is ready to forgive us. Through his affection and compassion, he tries to improve our lives. Not through justice-power but through forgiveness-power he wants to make us good citizens of the world. That is why the Holy Father is so unique.

INTERVIEWER: As I look around the rest of the world, I see more spirituality in other countries, especially in third world countries, than in America. I think there is more praying, more compassion, more of a desire to believe in something greater than physical being, whereas here in America I sense a lack of spirituality. What would you say to that?

SRI CHINMOY: I beg to be excused, but I cannot see eye to eye with you. You are an American, so you may say that Americans are not spiritual. But I feel that Americans are definitely spiritual. I happen to be a seeker of truth and a lover of God. I have been here in your country, America, for 33 years. During these 33 years, God has given me ample opportunity to be of service to the soul, to the heart and to the life of America. I have been to all the states, given talks at universities, answered questions and offered Peace Concerts, and I have found America to be quite receptive.

Everybody has his own way of thinking about spirituality. Some people are of the opinion that one is spiritual only if one enters into the Himalayan caves and gives up the worldly life. Again, others are of the opinion that we do not have to enter into the Himalayan caves; only we have to give up our desire-life and enter into the aspiration-life.

It is our desire-life that binds us. If we have one car, then we want to have two cars, three cars, four cars. One house is not enough; we want a second house and a third house. And each time we increase our desire-life, we bind ourselves tighter. But when we enter into the aspiration-life, we pray to God to give us peace of mind, light and bliss. Rather than try to exercise our supremacy over others, as we do in the desire-life, in the aspiration-life we try to become one, inseparably one, with the rest of the world. It is our oneness with others that gives us peace of mind and real satisfaction. And to achieve this we do not have to enter into the Himalayan caves or lead an isolated life. On the contrary, first we have to accept life as such and then we have to transform it. We have to transform our mind; we have to transform our life. We have to look forward or upward or dive deep within to bring to the fore our inner light.

Only then—only when we see, feel and grow into our inner light—can we become perfect citizens of the world. For this, America is an excellent place, just like any other country is, for an individual to practise spirituality.

INTERVIEWER: Well said! Absolutely! Thank you very much. That was beautiful.

Radio WJR
Detroit

INTERVIEWER: Our first guest is a gentleman who has written a book on Mother Teresa entitled *Mother Teresa: Humanity's Flower-Heart, Divinity's Fragrance-Soul*. He was on the telephone with Mother Teresa on his birthday just nine days before her passing. He is a prolific author, poet, artist, musician, athlete, etc. Sri Chinmoy joins us on WJR.

Sri Chinmoy, you mourn the loss of Mother Teresa, but you celebrate the work that she did and you carry on her memory in your book. I know it is important to you that we all remember her and her work and pick up where she left off.

SRI CHINMOY: It is absolutely true. We must try to follow in her footsteps.

INTERVIEWER: You held a special programme yesterday at the United Nations. Can you tell us about it?

SRI CHINMOY: At the United Nations, in the Dag Hammarskjöld Auditorium, we offered our prayers for her soul. The Ambassador of Bangladesh sponsored the occasion, and we prayed and sang. Also, some of the guests spoke very prayerfully about her. It was a prayerful service right from the beginning to the end. In 1975, at the same Dag Hammarskjöld Auditorium, I had the golden opportunity to be in her blessingful presence. I offered her a rose and she blessingfully accepted it.

INTERVIEWER: It is wonderful that you carry on her memory, and I am sure that it was exactly the kind of celebration Mother Teresa would have liked—with music and prayer. It is nice of you to share with us your book, *Mother Teresa: Humanity's Flower-Heart, Divinity's Fragrance-Soul,* taken from your time with her and your message of global peace, which is the same as hers.

SRI CHINMOY: We are all sailing in the same boat. Those who believe in peace, those who believe in world harmony, are all sailing in the same boat.

Radio WLW
Cincinnati

INTERVIEWER: Sri Chinmoy is on the line. Sir, first of all tell me, what was your relationship with Mother Teresa?

SRI CHINMOY: I am a great admirer of Mother Teresa. Her boundless affection and compassion I cherish and I shall forever cherish.

INTERVIEWER: In your book you have written several poems about her and several tributes. Do you think she had any idea while she was living how many people were aware of her work?

SRI CHINMOY: Yes, she was fully aware of the world's affection and admiration for her, but she did not care for it. She cared only for her prayerful service to her beloved Lord Jesus Christ in humanity. She did not care for name and fame. She cared only for one thing: her sleepless and breathless service to the poor and the needy.

INTERVIEWER: We had a priest on a week or two ago who had a chance to meet Mother Teresa in Calcutta. He said he was amazed at how nice this woman was. She was truly that way to everybody.

MY MOTHER OF COMPASSION, MY SISTER OF AFFECTION

SRI CHINMOY: She was for all with her affection, compassion, simplicity and humility. To stand before her was to feel one's own divine virtues—such as humility, patience and self-giving—coming to the fore.

Radio WGY
Albany

INTERVIEWER: The world reels at the loss of a frail little woman in her eighties who spent her entire life helping people that the rest of the world tried to turn its back on—Mother Teresa. And one of the people who knew this remarkable woman best is our guest this morning. Please welcome Sri Chinmoy.

Sir, we all know what a wonderful woman Mother Teresa was and how dedicated she was to helping the poor. But what would surprise us about Mother Teresa? Did she have a weakness for candy? Did she enjoy soccer? Tell us the personal things about her.

SRI CHINMOY: I can only tell you about my personal experience of Mother Teresa. For me she was the Mother of compassion and the Sister of affection. Quite a few times she said to me, "I pray for you every day. You must pray for me. I want you to come with me to China. China needs light." It was her affectionate and emotional demands and commands that she exercised upon me, and I shall always cherish her affection and her compassion.

INTERVIEWER: Sri Chinmoy is our guest this morning, author of the book *Mother Teresa: Humanity's Flower-Heart, Divinity's Fragrance-Soul,* and a friend of Mother Teresa. Now let's talk about you for just a minute. I know you grew up in India under British rule. What was that like, being a young man in India when it was the jewel in the crown of England?

SRI CHINMOY: I was brought up in a spiritual community, and I prayed for our independence. In 1947, on the 15th of August, God listened to the prayers of millions and millions of Indians. Recently, our present Prime Minister Gujral offered a momentous utterance. He said, "We are proud to say that Indian independence was won, not given." Many people are under the mistaken opinion that the British Government gave us our freedom.

INTERVIEWER: Oh, not at all. It was Mahatma Gandhi's campaign of peaceful resistance.

SRI CHINMOY: That is absolutely correct. Freedom was won, not given. Some think that the British showed a magnanimous heart. But it was not that. It was the sacrifices made by millions of people—the stupendous sacrifices, the sleepless and breathless sacrifices—that made independence possible.

INTERVIEWER: Did Gandhi's campaign of peaceful resistance influence your life at all? I ask because you are a Guru, a Teacher, and you've taught millions how to discover inner peace and fulfilment.

SRI CHINMOY: I was brought up in the Sri Aurobindo Ashram. There I prayed and meditated. So my life was influenced totally by prayer and meditation. I have the deepest admiration for Mahatma Gandhi. But his influence on our national life was mainly in the moral sphere. He practised and he advocated a moral code of life. In my case, from my prayer-life and meditation-life I try to get messages from within. I solely depend on my prayer-life and meditation-life.

Mother Teresa-Charity-Critics Are Mental Cases!

THE CONCEPT OF CHARITY

Sri Chinmoy gave the following talk on 11 September 1997.

Some so-called spiritual people sneer at the concept of charity. They say that we have to go to the root cause of ignorance in order to heal the sufferings of humanity. They feel that the answer lies in self-perfection and not in charity. According to their philosophy, the poor and the sick must endure suffering for certain karmic reasons. Therefore, it is God's responsibility to take care of them, since He created them.

If you carry this philosophy to its inevitable conclusion and say that it is not necessary to provide services for those who suffer, then there should be no doctors or hospitals. There will be no foundation for the existence of medical science.

Fortunately, most spiritual paths include and encompass the ideal of charity in a broad sense. They feel that charity is a part of spirituality because it is based on self-giving. The expansion of our normal consciousness in various ways may take the form of charity. We see that somebody needs our concern, somebody needs treatment, somebody needs love, and we try to offer what we have and what we are lovingly, if not unconditionally.

From the highest point of view, I fully agree that charity and philanthropy are not the answer to alleviate humanity's sufferings. In order to serve God inside our fellow human beings, we must first know what God's Will is. The Saviour Christ taught us to pray, "Let Thy Will be done." There can be no higher prayer than this. It is through prayer and meditation that we will come to realise and know what His Will is. Only a God-realised soul can ask God directly whom he should help and in what way.

But before we achieve this state of oneness with God, we are bound to pass through hundreds of human incarnations. While we are waiting to hear God's Voice and to receive His inner Messages, must we just wait and do nothing? Suppose we see somebody dying in the street, will we wait for God's Command before we go and help that person? Will we argue with ourselves and say, "Obviously he deserves this fate. In his previous incarnation he must have done many bad things"?

Where is our conscience? Where is our common sense? Did God not give us a heart to identify ourselves with the suffering of others? If somebody is in dire need of my assistance, will I not go and help that person if I have the capacity? Similarly, when I am in desperate straits, other kind-hearted people will come to my rescue. If we do not help one another like this, then what kind of society are we living in?

Suppose the person who is suffering is a close relative of ours. At that time we do not care for philosophy. When a near and dear one is suffering, we discard our philosophical detachment. We immediately run to help them. We are not interested in knowing the root cause of the problem, which may be something they did in a previous incarnation. We are only concerned with the present. When our mother or father falls ill, we will stay at the hospital round the clock because of our love and concern for them. We pray that God in the form of the doctor will be able to do the needful and cure them.

When we expand our consciousness, we come to see all of humanity as one family. We come to feel that we do not belong just to our immediate family, just to our own little village or to our own country. No, we belong to the whole world and the whole world belongs to us. We claim the whole world as our oneness-family. So if someone is suffering in our larger family, naturally we will try to help that person. The spirituality that makes us shut our heart-door to others is a very narrow kind of spirituality. Genuine spirituality helps us to expand our self-offering.

In Mother Teresa's case, she went one step further. She saw inside the poor, the sick and the dying the living presence of Jesus Christ. That is why she was able to serve the poorest of the poor with such humility and love. Some self-styled critics of Mother Teresa claim that she did not follow a truly spiritual life. They declare that her life of service cannot be compared to a life of prayer and worship.

Swami Vivekananda, the giant Hindu spiritual figure, fell victim to the same criticism when he urged his brother-disciples to practise the life of service. He told them: If you really love God the Creator, then you must serve God the creation, the suffering humanity.

Mother Teresa's life of dedicated service to the poor, the sick and the dying was her prayer in action. No one who came into contact with her could fail to observe that Jesus was always on her tongue and in her heart. At every moment, she prayed for God's Blessings. And God did shower His Blessings upon her in boundless measure.

While it is true that Mother Teresa's exemplary life embodied charity in its highest form, it is equally true that many people perform acts of charity with an altogether different attitude. If one person has ten dollars and he gives away five pennies to a poor person, he may feel that he has done an act of charity, that he has made a tremendous sacrifice. Or he may donate some discarded, unwanted clothes to those whom he considers to be objects of pity.

The clothes may not even be useable, but he will feel that he has done someone a great favour, like a king giving alms to a beggar. Although the king has vast wealth, he gives just a tiny portion of it and he feels that is more than enough.

There is a great difference between charity that is based on limited self-giving and charity that is based on unconditional self-offering. Unconditional self-offering comes from the integral, entire being, whereas limited self-giving comes from an infinitesimal portion of our existence.

In limited self-giving we feel that we are superior and others are inferior. We may pity somebody, but while doing so we remain on the Himalayan heights and we see the person to whom we are showing pity at the bottom of a chasm. We stand millions of miles higher than the heartbreaking reality of the other person.

When charity is based on unconditional self-offering, on the other hand, we feel that the poor and the sick are like our little brothers and sisters. In a family, there can be no superiority and no inferiority. It is all oneness. The older brother will share what he has with his little brother, not because he pities him, but because he has compassion for him. When we show compassion, at that time our whole being becomes one with the suffering of others. If somebody is poverty-stricken and we offer our compassion, we become one with his poverty itself. We just come to him and become one with his problems.

This is what Mother Teresa did on a daily basis. She herself braved unimaginable poverty and hardship in order to become one with the poor people of India. It is a far cry from her self-offering to the charitable donations of big businessmen who are seeking a way to evade taxes. Do they see, like Mother Teresa, the living presence of Jesus Christ inside the poor? Never, never. I do not wish to decry the contributions of wealthy people. There are some who have very large hearts and who genuinely wish to help the world-family to become happy and progressive. By not hoarding their wealth in a selfish way they are definitely elevating the consciousness of mankind and inspiring others to follow their example.

But the utter, unconditional self-offering that we find in the life of Mother Teresa will have no equal. I am reminded of an incident that occurred when Mother Teresa first opened up her Home for the Dying, Nirmal Hriday, at Kalighat in Calcutta. Some members of the local community stood against her. They believed that she was trying to convert everybody from Hinduism to Christianity. The local police chief agreed to go and investigate the complaints. As soon as he entered Nirmal Hriday, he saw that Mother Teresa was bending over a dying man and pulling out the worms from his body. The stench was so unbearable that the police chief hastily left the building. When he returned to the people who had lodged the complaint, he said, "You are all so undivine! You talk about God, but you do nothing to help humanity. If I ask Mother Teresa to leave, will any of you take her place and look after this dying man? Never! I do not see her as a mere human being. If she is not God, then who is God?"

Mother Teresa taught us that if somebody is standing at our heart-door, we should not allow that person to wait outside like a beggar. We should immediately embrace him and give him what we have and what we are. Our complete self-offering to the divine in him is nothing other than charity in its purest sense of the term, bordering on real spirituality.

I strongly feel that Mother Teresa's inspiration-light will spread to countless people in various levels of society the world over. As they come to learn about the life and work of this Himalayan-height saint, they will be filled with the inspiration to think more of others than of themselves and to offer their heart's boundless love and concern to each and every member of our oneness-world-family.

To conclude, Princess Diana also sailed in the same boat as Mother Teresa towards the same destination, the Golden Shore. Alas, Princess Diana's life-tree was snapped before it could reach its highest height with foliage, flowers, fragrance and nourishing fruits. No wonder why Mother Teresa most affectionately and most proudly claimed Diana as her daughter. When Mother and daughter met for the last time on June 18th in the Bronx, New York, their mutual love and affection can only be felt and never be described.

— Postscript: Letter from Sister Nirmala —

+
LDM

54A, A.J.C. Bose Road, Calcutta 700016.

"As long as you did it to one of these My least brethren. You did it to Me"

Dear Sri Chinmoy,

I am so grateful to God for you, for the love and joy you have shared with our dearest Mother over the years, particularly that evening in New York - that was heavenly.

Mother was always delighted to meet you. Thank you for the gifts, pictures, and beautiful frames you so lovingly and delicately presented to Mother. Thank you for the mandolin in remembrance of Mother's childhood. Thank you also for more pictures of Mother you are sending to us. I love it so much, so do all our sisters.

Love and friendship are God's gifts - a sign of His presence among us. Mother always appreciated your presence and goodness to her.

Though we all miss our dearest Mother's physical presence, we know that her spirit will continue to live and grow in all who reach out in love, respect, compassion and presence to our needy neighbour.

The medicines you sent us have arrived, thank you for them.

Please pray much for us, so that we continue God's work - all for His glory and the good of the poorest of the poor.

God bless you
M. Nirmala MC

Mother,
The sorrowful earth-planet
Has a special treasure-home,
And that home
Is your compassion-heart.